COME, LET US WORSHIP GOD

Come, Let Us Worship God

A HANDBOOK OF PRAYERS FOR LEADERS OF WORSHIP

By
David M. Currie

THE WESTMINSTER PRESS
Philadelphia

Book Design by Dorothy Alden Smith

First Edition

Published by The Westminster Press®
Philadelphia, Pennsylvania

PRINTED IN THE UNITED STATES OF AMERICA

9 8 7 6 5 4 3 2 1

Library of Congress Cataloging in Publication Data

Currie, David M 1918–
Come, let us worship God.

1. Pastoral prayers. I. Title.
BV250.C87 242'.89'2 77–6808
ISBN 0–664–24757–1

CONTENTS

FOREWORD

This collection of prayers and calls to worship has grown out of the performance of my weekly privilege of leading persons in the corporate worship of God. The calls to worship do not follow the traditional form, since they do not use a selected verse of Scripture. I came to this style of call to worship in an earlier pastorate. Disturbed I long had been by the standard calls, sung and spoken:

> "The Lord is in his holy temple;
> let all the earth keep silence before him,"

usually followed immediately by the blast of the organ and the singing of a hymn; or,

> "O come, let us worship and bow down,
> let us kneel before the Lord, our Maker."

Few would "bow down," and none in the Reformed tradition of worship expected to kneel in public!

Many persons begin a service of public worship with the statement:

> "Let us worship God,"

and there is good precedent for doing so. Such beginning seems to me abrupt. These stark words somehow leave me cold. They gave me an idea, however: Why not begin by saying something about the God whom we are gathered to worship? So I began to try to "teach theology" in calls to public worship.

The prayers of confession developed later in a parish that wished to have included weekly a prayer of confession in its order of corporate worship. Years ago I heard Bishop Pike of the Episcopal Church express impatience with the "general confession" included in *The Book of Common Prayer.* He observed that it was too general to be significant and helpful—and that it made no acknowledgment of indiscretions at recent cocktail parties or on the golf course, where many Episcopalians spend much of their time.

So I tried to prepare a different prayer for each Sunday, hoping that over the weeks some sinning apropos to each worshiper would be acknowledged and confessed. The phrase "all too often" regularly appears, giving persons an "out" who do not feel that the named sin is one they committed recently. I have avoided the use of the more standard phrasing: "We all have sinned by . . . ," which suggests that everyone is equally guilty for all sorts and conditions of sin confessed in the prayer prayed in unison.

An article in *The Presbyterian Outlook* raised questions in my mind about the declaration of pardon now found in many services of corporate worship. One question was: "If persons have not individually been moved to sincere repentance and earnest desire for amendment of their sinful ways, is it theologically sound or psychologically proper to declare that their sins are forgiven?"

So I tried to develop a sequence in which a statement of the likelihood of our sinning is followed by a prayer of confession that includes a request for help toward new obedience. Then follows a declaration of God's desire and ability to forgive those who confess, repent, and seek his help to live in faith and obedience. Examples of this sequence are included.

I am indebted to the following for their assistance in the preparation of this book: Dr. Aubrey N. Brown, Editor, *The Presbyterian Outlook,* whose editorial judgment gave many of these calls and prayers their first publication, and am grateful for permission to reprint the ones that appeared there; the congregations of the First Presbyterian Churches of Durham, North Carolina, and of Corpus Christi and Seguin, Texas, for whose use these calls and prayers came into being; Thomas W. and Jeannette R. Currie, from whose lips I first heard God addressed in prayer and by whose daily example in praying I was nurtured in two-way communication with God; the agents of The Westminster Press, whose discretion it was to offer this Handbook to those who lead in Christian worship.

The Handbook is offered with the hope that it will enable leaders of corporate Christian worship to manifest the awe and adoration proper to those who present themselves before the Sovereign of all creation and Author of our salvation.

D.M.C.

CALLS TO WORSHIP AND OPENING PRAYERS

CALLS TO WORSHIP, OPENING PRAYERS

God, whom we are gathered to worship,
knows your family tree, all the way back to Adam and Eve;
knows full well the links in your chromosome chain;
knows the prints on your fingers,
the convolutions of your ears; and
knows the memories and hopes
that live within your cerebral cortex.
Come, let us worship God, and to him let us pray.

O God, our Father,
your knowledge of each of us is infinite, and your love for each of us is boundless;
you place us within human families, and incorporate us into the beloved household of faith:
We yield ourselves to your providence and grace.
We rejoice that you have called us from our varying human backgrounds to be brothers and sisters together in faith and devotion.
We renew our commitments to each other, to mothers and fathers, to sisters and brothers, to neighbors and acquaintances, through Jesus Christ, our Savior, elder brother, companion.
Together we address you in trust as Jesus taught disciples to pray, for themselves and for others:

Our Father, who art in heaven, hallowed . . .

God, whom we gather to worship,
watched with anticipation as Columbus "sailed the ocean blue in fourteen hundred ninety-two,"
followed with interest Magellan's sailing around the world, and
shared the excitement as a human being first set foot on the moon.
Come, let us worship God, and to him let us pray.

O God, our Father,
you designed the whole universe and placed in it human beings to have dominion, acting as trusted tenants:
Direct each of us in our adventures of living,
teach us more constantly to rejoice in your sovereignty,
enable us to deepen our sense of kinship with all human beings,
sustain us in our endeavors to be faithful, productive tenants.
We bless and praise you for all faithful persons, throughout the centuries, who have created beauty,
increased goodness,
advanced faith.
For the whole world, and for all persons in it, we pray to you, together, as Jesus taught disciples:

Our Father, who art in heaven, hallowed . . .

God, whom we gather to worship,
gave the mockingbird its melodious repertoire,
gave the wild flowers their brilliant hues,
gave the moon its silvery gleam, and
gives persons reasons to laugh with joy,
surely merits our praise and adoration for bountiful mercies continually showered upon us.
Come, let us worship God, and to him let us pray.

O God, our Father,
we praise you for jobs to do, and for the strength to do them;
we praise you for problems, and for the wisdom and imagination to solve them;
we praise you for adventures of action and intellect, and for the courage and persistence to achieve the good;
we praise you for your love which sustains us,
for your judgment which disciplines us,
for your balm which heals us,
for your Spirit which makes us fruitful.
Accept our praise, and hear us as we pray to you the prayer Jesus gave disciples:

Our Father, who art in heaven, hallowed . . .

God, whom we gather to worship,
especially blesses multitudes of persons through grand-mothers
who knit and crochet and do needlepoint
and sew delightful treasures,
who baby-sit with compassion and loving attention,
who have time to listen and time to reminisce,
who bring titillating surprises and soothing embraces,
who read to us, sing and go shopping with us, speak up for us.
Come, let us worship God, and to him let us pray.

O God, our Father,
you devise so many channels through which your graces flow to us, and
you so frequently select grandmothers as such arteries:
We praise you for our extended biological families, and
we give thanks for our even larger intergenerational family within this congregation.
Turn us sensitively toward one another, that vibrations of love and affection will rise in a symphony of harmony and joy.
Let swell such empathy and compassion that each one of us will be engulfed in love and hope.
And that such bliss may come to every person upon the globe, we earnestly pray the prayer Jesus gave disciples:

Our Father, who art in heaven, hallowed . . .

God, whom we gather to worship,
worked his purposes through
buck-passing Adam and Eve,
enterprising Noah,
stolid Abraham,
conniving Jacob,
placid Isaac,
egotistical Joseph,
stammering Moses,
sorrowful Samuel,
boisterous David,
aloof Elijah,
diligent Ruth,
charming Esther,
courageous Deborah,
promiscuous Rahab,
urbane Isaiah,
weeping Jeremiah,
cuckold Hosea,
and hosts of other diverse persons.
Come, let us worship God, and to him let us pray.

O God, our Father,
thank you for the marvelous variety of persons you create.
Thank you for your trust and confidence in all kinds of persons.
Thank you for your patience and skill in working your purposes through such persons as we.
Give us wisdom and grace to associate in great undertakings, for your goals, with all sorts and conditions of persons.
To make your work easier and our work exciting, more earnestly than ever we pray, for ourselves and for others, the prayer Jesus taught disciples to pray:

Our Father, who art in heaven, hallowed . . .

God, whom we gather to worship,
is not unmindful of golfers—their problems and their pleasures:
whistling drives coming calmly to rest in the fairway,
high-flying approach shots snuggling down on the greens,
slow-rolling putts which wend their way into the cup;
as well as
slices and hooks bouncing about in the rough,
"look-ups" and "whiff" strokes, with calamitous results,
water balls splashing down into oblivion.
Come, let us worship God, and to him let us pray.

O God, our Father,
we remember with pleasure the beauties of courses we have played;
we recollect with joy low scores and spectacular shots;
we are grateful for good fellowship and shared rejoicings.
Give us equal zest for our daily labors,
equal attention to details necessary for improvement,
equal resolve to "stay at it," to "do better next time."
On our regular jobs help us to assume proper responsibility for getting things done well: eyes steady, grip firm, concentration fixed, follow-through never forgotten.
And what we desire and work for ourselves, we ask for others, too, as we pray to you, together, as Jesus taught disciples:

Our Father, who art in heaven, hallowed . . .

God, whom we gather to worship,
watches with interest surfers riding the breakers,
fishers casting in hope,
beachcombers scanning the tide-lands,
sunbathers basking and baking,
sailors jibbing and quartering the wind,
swimmers jumping the waves,
vendors plying their trade, and
lifeguards checking on the milling throng.
Come, let us worship God, and to him let us pray.

O God, our Father,
thank you for such a fascinating place as the seaside,
with its myriad water creatures,
with its plethora of shells and sand and plants,
with its rhythmic tides and shifting breezes.
Thank you for occasions to enjoy such glories of your creation,
for other persons to share the pleasure, and
for those who are on the lookout for our safety.
Let the sea speak to us of the vastness and power of your grace.
Let the abundance of sand remind us of all the persons you love.
Let the lifeguards remind us of your everlasting concern for our salvation through Jesus, who taught all disciples to pray:

Our Father, who art in heaven, hallowed . . .

God, whom we gather to worship,
watches with interest as we
make our contracts in bridge,
wipe out our opponents in checkers,
get all the way home in backgammon or parcheesi,
outscore all others in dominoes and cribbage,
bluff our way through in poker, and
checkmate a rival in chess.
He is acquainted with all the other games people play—
with, or against, one another.
Come, let us worship God, and to him let us pray.

O God, our Father,
you cause us to be stimulated by competition,
you know our ambition to win, and
you see through all our deceits and dissemblings:
Keep us mindful of your desire
for us also to be helpful, one to another,
for us to aid others to succeed in wholesome living,
for us to rejoice in others' victories over trouble and sorrow.
Fix afresh our attention on Jesus,
who lived his earthly life and died his earthly death so others would receive victory.
And, to this end, we pray to you as Jesus taught disciples to pray:

Our Father, who art in heaven, hallowed . . .

God, whom we gather to worship,
notes with interest as persons reach out to one another
by direct distance dialing, CB chatter, ham radio CQ's;
by teletype, WATS line, FTD florists;
by SOS and Mayday signals; and
by telepathic impulses.
He, too, reaches out to you,
to tell of his love—for you;
to deliver his promises—for you;
to give directions—to you;
to present commendations—to you;
to deliver you from evil.
Come, let us worship God, and to him let us pray.

O God, our Father,
amid all the pulsing messages that impinge upon us, help us tune in your frequency.
Praise to you for your persistence, even when on our number you receive a busy signal,
even when we are chitchatting blithely about mundane matters.
Praise to you for loving us so much that you sent Jesus to deliver, in person, your word for us.
Help us to tune in your clear channel for a splendid two-way conversation during our service of worship—and we begin by addressing you as Jesus taught disciples to do:

Our Father, who art in heaven, hallowed . . .

God, whom we gather to worship,
has blessed us through faithful Sunday school teachers,
has comforted us through tender ministries of loving circles,
has challenged us through advisers to youth groups,
has inspired us through choir directors and organists,
has led us well through insightful church leaders . . .
Come, let us worship God, and to him let us pray.

O God, our Father,
we bless and praise you for the manifold benefits accorded us because you have incorporated us within the extended family of this congregation.
We give thanks for every opportunity made available to us to be channels of your grace to others within this fellowship.
Inspire us, one and all, to reach out in effective love to enfold more and more persons into this loving, redeeming, commissioning communion, so that soon all persons everywhere will join with us in praying as Jesus taught disciples:

Our Father, who art in heaven, hallowed . . .

God, whom we gather to worship,
has watched persons here blessed in baptism,
couples here united in marriage,
celebrations here on the occasion of physical death,
pilgrims here sustained by grace through the Lord's Supper,
petitioning persons here comforted, directed, answered through prayer, and
inquirers here enlightened by his Word rightly read and diligently preached and attentively received.
Come, let us worship God, and to him let us pray.

O God, our Father,
you have given sacraments, rites, liturgies as vehicles of your multifaceted mercies:
We are profoundly grateful for every support given us in crucial times.
Let each baptism, each marriage, each memorial celebration have pristine freshness.
Let each sharing of the Lord's Supper strengthen our bonds of devotion and our commitment to self-giving service.
Refresh us anew with precious promises, restraining warnings, glorious good news from your Word, proclaimed and heard.
And, once again, let miracles flow through prayer as we join in praying as Jesus taught disciples to pray to you, for themselves and for others:

Our Father, who art in heaven, hallowed . . .

God, whom we gather to worship,
is aware of the gifts of sacrifice and love that went into the building of this place of worship;
recalls the hosts of persons
who have ushered worshipers to their places,
who have sung the gospel and lifted prayers in harmony,
who have served as prophets in the pulpit,
who have presided over baptisms, and
who have served the sacred meal.
He affirms that other persons have labored, and that we have entered into their labors.
Come, let us worship God, and to him let us pray.

O God, our Father,
we rejoice in recollections of the hosts of saints (sinners saved by your grace) who have preceded us in the fellowship of this congregation.
We seek to honor the heritage entrusted to us by them through putting to work talents you have given us.
We fervently pray that those in succeeding years will be able to look back in gratitude at our stewardship of the mysteries of your providence.
We join, once again, in offering to you that prayer which disciples, across the centuries, have prayed together:

Our Father, who art in heaven, hallowed . . .

God, whom we gather to worship,
gave radar to bats
before human beings discovered the principle,
gave sonar to porpoises
before human beings developed the technique,
gave navigational skills to birds and fish
before human beings designed chart and compass.
Come, let us worship God, and to him let us pray.

O God, our Father,
we stand in awe of the marvelous intricacy,
the amazing harmony,
the astounding wonders within your creation.
Keep us ever mindful that we too are intertwined, by your providence, within the fascinating fabric of the ecosystem.
Help us to remember, always, your continuing labors for all creation to achieve renewed harmony through allegiance to the Lordship of Jesus;
and to that end we pray:

Our Father, who art in heaven, hallowed . . .

God, whom we gather to worship,
knows each of you intimately:
those who have loved ones gravely ill;
those who are joyfully in love;
those who greet each day with gladness and expectancy;
those who stagger under burdens heavy and wearisome;
those who are frightfully lonely, exceedingly apprehensive;
those who are vigorously active, confidently confronting challenges;
those who are marking time awaiting legal maturity, desirous of personal freedom.
Not only does God know you intimately, but he also is ready and able to minister to you effectively in this very hour.
Come, let us worship God, and to him let us pray.

O God, our Father,
your mercies are new every morning, fresh every evening;
your arms are not shortened so that you cannot save;
you are eager to give the Holy Spirit to those who ask:
Reach into each life with refreshing love and useful gifts.
Work miracles of healing and salvation;
lighten many burdens and dramatically strengthen burden bearers.
Open the lonely to words of greeting and gestures of love.
Energize afresh the achievers of good;
stay the tempted and grant them new and wholesome desires.
Challenge and commission the eager to self-giving service.
Keenly conscious of our own condition and seeking to be sensitive to others, we lift to you, together, the prayer Jesus gave disciples:

Our Father, who art in heaven, hallowed . . .

Rest assured:
God, whom we gather to worship,
in his glorious goodness is ready and able to respond personally to you in your particular need and mood.
Some are here ready to shout with the psalmist:
"Make a joyful noise unto the Lord. . . ."
Some are here who are echoing the anguish of the psalmist:
"Out of the depths have I cried unto thee, O Lord. Lord, hear my voice. . . ."
Some are here looking for guidance and direction from the Word of God:
"More to be desired are they than gold, . . .
Sweeter also than honey and the honeycomb. . . ."
Some are here with passionate longing for fellowship with God:
"As the hart panteth after the water brooks,
So panteth my soul after thee, O God. . . ."
Come, let us worship God, and to him let us pray.

O God, our Father,
we are here, rather than
in bed, at the beach, in front of the television,
at work in yard or kitchen, traveling on the highway,
strolling the golf links, or skiing on water or snow.
We are here, expectant that you will be helpful to us.
Receive our praise and thanksgiving.
Grant us forgiveness, comfort, mercy, and health.
Enlighten us in our inquiring.
Challenge us with new revelation from your Word.
Enfold us once again within your household of fellowship and love.
Equip us to be useful to you in answering the prayer Jesus gave disciples:

Our Father, who art in heaven, hallowed . . .

God, whom we gather to worship,
caused a manger and a cross to speak eloquently of his presence among us and of his love for human beings; and even today he pursues his gracious purposes alongside contemporary Caesars, Herods, and Pilates.
Come, let us worship God, and to him let us pray.

O God, our Father,
keep our faith in you updated.
Let the words—read, sung, and spoken here today—
excite us with the assurance that
TODAY you so love the world
that Jesus is active within it among all persons,
so that whoever believes in him will not perish
but will have, from you, wholesome, everlasting life.
Confident anew of your participation in the affairs of our day,
we pray to you as Jesus taught disciples:

Our Father, who art in heaven, hallowed . . .

God, whom we gather to worship,
still works wonders;
has better ideas;
gives you round-the-clock protection;
makes the going great;
keeps you feeling fresh all day; and
is the real thing.
If these statements cause you to remember phrases from current television commercials, that's all right:
for God cared enough to send the very best: his own Son, whom we have come to know as Lord and to accept as personal Savior.
To any person here who has not accepted Jesus as Lord and Savior, we declare:
"Try him, you'll like him!"
He will do vastly more for you than settle your stomach.
Come, let us worship God, and to him let us pray.

O God, our Father,
we turn again to you in adoration, praise, and thanksgiving!
We celebrate your faithful, righteous, and powerful sovereignty over all.
We rejoice in your merciful provision for our healing and wholeness in Jesus.
We give thanks to you for the trust of life, talents for serving, capacity for loving, by which we are blessed every day.
To you we lift up our hearts and voices, praying, for ourselves and for others, as Jesus taught disciples to pray:

Our Father, who art in heaven, hallowed . . .

God, whom we gather to worship,
provides for his children short admonitions for proper behavior:
revere parents,
no murder,
no adultery,
no stealing,
no lying,
no jealousy,

love God,
love neighbor,
love self.

He sent Jesus to demonstrate, on earth, in ordinary society, the grandeur—and the agony—of such living.
He continues to provide the Holy Spirit to be our Counselor, Advocate, and Sustainer for such living in our complex society.
Come, let us worship God, and to him let us pray.

O God, our Father,
you have loved each of us into being,
you are actively at work today in your creation, and
you judge righteously, forgive mercifully, and redeem graciously:
Fix anew in our minds and hearts and wills your commands for our personal behavior, and
grant us fresh assurance of your forgiveness of our sin confessed, and of your power to remake us for righteousness.
And, for ourselves and for others, we pray as Jesus taught disciples:

Our Father, who art in heaven, hallowed . . .

God, whom we gather to worship,
followed with interest the rendezvous in space of Soviet and American persons—with all its teamwork, telemetry, and technical skill:
five persons monitored across space for heartbeat, respiration, voice;
five persons receiving across space "checkout" on programs of works;
five persons aided across space in solving problems unexpectedly encountered.
Even so, God, whom we worship, has forever had each one of us under comprehensive observation—
monitoring our vital signs,
counseling us on scheduled work, and
being immediately available to help us solve unexpected problems.
Come, let us worship God, and to him let us pray.

Almighty God, creator of the universe and its sustainer,
in gracious love you sent Jesus on a glorious mission to earth, and
you have each one of us under your omniscient surveillance:
Accept our profound gratitude and abundant praise;
fix our attention on your plans for our work;
counsel us when the unexpected happens;
keep us mindful of the great crowd of witnesses watching our performance, hopeful and confident.
And to you, whose concern reaches out to every person on the globe, we pray as Jesus taught disciples to pray, for themselves and for others:

Our Father, who art in heaven, hallowed . . .

God, whom we gather to worship,
loved into being Abraham Lincoln, and
molded the winsome, steadfast character of Robert E. Lee;
gives evidence of his strong confidence in human families
by trusting the infant Jesus to the keeping of Joseph and Mary.
Come, let us worship God, and to him let us pray.

O God, our Father,
help us to labor, now and always, for wholesome homes for all children:
for children of all skin colors,
for children of all economic conditions,
for children of every nation,
for children of crowded city and of lonesome countryside.
And, by your saving mercy and marvelous providence,
may all children, and their parents, come to address you in trust and in love as Jesus taught disciples to address you in prayer:

Our Father, who art in heaven, hallowed . . .

God, whom we gather to worship,
can let his wisdom be known and applied
in legislative halls,
in ad men's deliberations,
in merchants' trade marts;
can have his works of mercy and compassion done
through churches,
through United Fund agencies,
through workmen's compensation procedures.
Come, let us worship God, and to him let us pray.

O God, our Father,
deliver us from ever thinking your interests are limited to Sundays, and more especially to what transpires within sanctuaries dedicated to your worship.
Alert us anew to your pervasive concerns,
to your multifarious avenues of action,
to your desire for the salvation of persons,
so they can be commissioned to holy service.
Keep us attuned to the social, political, and economic implications of the prayer Jesus gave disciples:

Our Father, who art in heaven, hallowed . . .

God, whom we gather to worship,
is praised by the singing to the accompaniment of pipe organs, jungle drums, staccato pianos, strummed guitars, Salvation Army bands;
is praised by such diverse persons as Mahalia Jackson, George Beverly Shea, Merle Haggard.
Be encouraged today to add your voice to joyful noise lifted in praise to God.
Come, let us worship God, and to him let us pray.

O God, our Father,
though our "joyful noise" may not be as melodious as that of songbirds, or not as harmonious as that of a barbershop quartet,
we will offer in gladness the best praise of which we are capable—with our voices, our hands, our feet, our hearts.
And to our joyfulness we add, here and now, the pulsing prayer Jesus gave disciples to pray to you:

Our Father, who art in heaven, hallowed . . .

God, whom we gather to worship,
overshadows with his providence
a nation in its crises,
a satellite in its orbit,
a lonely freshman in college,
a young couple in love.
He makes his wisdom available to
the President in the White House,
the business executive in the office,
the union steward on the job,
the scientist in the laboratory,
the housewife in the kitchen.
Come, let us worship God, and to him let us pray.

O God, our Father,
Sovereign over all, yet nearer than hands or feet,
closer even than our breathing;
wise beyond our comprehension, yet able and willing
to give wisdom to aid us in any present perplexity:
Refresh us each today with sound confidence and useful knowledge.
With thanksgiving and expectancy we pray to you as Jesus taught disciples to pray, for themselves and for others:

Our Father, who art in heaven, hallowed . . .

God, whom we gather to worship,
gives us a sense of time and of the awareness that each moment is precious and pregnant with possibilities;
planned for human beings to be born into families, nurtured by families, and liberated by families into useful personhood; and
structured the universe itself into rhythmic movement, giving us day and night, for working and sleeping,
for worship and labor.
Come, let us worship God, and to him let us pray.

O God, our Father,
present with us, here and now, in this place of sanctuary,
direct us as we reckon up our inventories of resources and responsibilities,
as we rejoice in family fellowship renewed, and
as we seek guidance for the new "year of our Lord."
We praise you for teaching us that, as Sovereign over all time and space, you still want each person to know and love you as Father, and to pray to you, together, as Jesus taught disciples to pray:

Our Father, who art in heaven, hallowed . . .

God, whom we gather to worship,
knows carpenters, electricians, plumbers, bricklayers, suppliers, contractors, and foremen;
accompanies, when asked, the ill, the bereaved, the perplexed; and can aid those who labor, who manage, who invest.
Come, let us worship God, and to him let us pray.

O God, our Father,
we seek to pattern our worship of you after that of Jesus,
who was a carpenter, who knew perplexity,
who experienced bereavement, and
who worked in the confidence of doing your will.
To that end, we are bold to address you in prayer as Jesus taught disciples to pray:

Our Father, who art in heaven, hallowed . . .

Rest assured:
God, whom we gather to worship,
understands the melodic chant of the tobacco auctioneer,
the cryptic orders of the investment broker,
the "Please, may I help you" of the retail salesperson.
He is not absent from
the excitement of football games,
the full-throttle roar of the auto racetrack,
the give-and-take of a stimulating classroom.
Come, let us worship God, and to him let us pray.

O God, our Father,
our worship of you is inspired by Jesus, sent in your love to people in bustling city and quiet countryside,
in places of learning and the raucous marketplace,
in the security of homes and the stress of courtrooms.
Our prayers to you follow the pattern of the prayer Jesus gave disciples:

Our Father, who art in heaven, hallowed . . .

God, whom we gather to worship,
designed the massive roar of the blizzard gale
and the lilting laughter of a little baby;
can cause the whole horizon to be bathed in crimson at sunset,
and gently spots the throat of a hummingbird with ruby;
has revealed his will and way to massive men like Moses
and to simple persons like Mary of Nazareth.
Come, let us worship God, and to him let us pray.

O God, our Father,
God beyond all other gods,
God nearer than all others,
God, our Father, we worship you, we adore you,
we bless and praise you.
And, as Jesus of Nazareth, your great self-disclosure, taught disciples, so with love and expectancy we pray to you:

Our Father, who art in heaven, hallowed . . .

God, whom we gather to worship,
has knowledge of you more detailed than any physician's history, any credit bureau record, or any FBI dossier;
has apperception more penetrating than any radio telescope; and
has mercy which goes far beyond even a mother's compassion.
Come, let us worship God, and to him let us pray.

O God, our Father,
you are aware of our performance as we
prepare our tax returns,
pull the levers in our polling places,
decide in jury rooms,
vote in board meetings or on honor councils; and
you judge us in the discharge of all our responsibilities:
Give us the courage to be faithful, day by day, to the Lordship of Jesus, who taught us to pray for the coming, on earth, of your kingdom of righteousness, mercy, and love:

Our Father, who art in heaven, hallowed . . .

God, whom we gather to worship,
rides with the police on their beat,
sits with the disc jockey in the studio, and
accompanies you in your daily rounds.
Come, let us worship God, and to him let us pray.

O God,
you were hymned by the psalmist as Shepherd,
and described by prophets as King:
Let each of us know you as Companion
in the plant and in the classroom,
in the hospital and in the commercial office,
beside the sink and on the golf links.
Be to each of us Judge and Counselor,
Boss and Fellow Laborer, and
Savior of our souls.
With gratitude for all past mercies,
and with high hopes for future blessings,
we pray to you, together, as Jesus taught disciples to pray:

Our Father, who art in heaven, hallowed . . .

God, whom we gather to worship,
is worshiped this day in Brisbane, Manila, Santiago, Kinshasa, Budapest, Saigon, Bombay;
is acknowledged on the coins you use all week;
is acclaimed in the pledge of allegiance to the flag of this nation; and
is acquainted fully with your joys and sorrows, with your triumphs and defeats.
Come, let us worship God, and to him let us pray.

O God,
you understand Spanish and Portuguese, French and Arabic, Hindustani and Slavic;
you know corporate management, tribal powwows, and congregational deliberations:
Look with wisdom and love upon each one of us;
comfort us who are sorrowful,
strengthen us who are fatigued,
enlighten us who are inquiring, and
save any of us who are lost.
As we begin to sing your praise, hear your Word, and pledge ourselves anew to your kingdom among human beings, we join our hearts and voices in praying to you as Jesus taught disciples to pray:

Our Father, who art in heaven, hallowed . . .

God, whom we gather to worship,
knows the data on report cards,
is acquainted with business balance sheets, and
marks the progress of each of us toward Christlikeness.
Come, let us worship God, and to him let us pray.

O God,
you are record keeper and judge;
before you nations are judged on righteousness, justice, and mercy, and
by you persons are judged on service, love, obedience, and trust:
We worship you.
Were there not forgiveness with you,
terror would be our attitude in your presence.
Speak to us this day of repentance, contrition, confession
. . . and of the forgiveness, renewal, and healing you have
for those who pray, sincerely, as Jesus taught disciples:

Our Father, who art in heaven, hallowed . . .

God, whom we gather to worship,
set the timetable of the tides,
determined the speed of light, and
knows the appointed rhythms of your life:
joys and sorrows, victories and defeats,
days of vigor and seasons of fatigue.
Come, let us worship God, and to him let us pray.

O God,
we celebrate your handiwork in the created universe, and
we acknowledge your providence in human affairs.
Confront each of us afresh this hour.
Let us hear your Word with expectancy;
let us sing your praise with joy;
let us resolve anew to obey more consistently your commands and claim more resolutely your promises.
Thanks to you for your self-revelation through Jesus, who walked the paths of Palestine, demonstrating to persons your will and nature.
As he taught disciples, so, together, we pray to you:

Our Father, who art in heaven, hallowed . . .

God, whom we gather to worship,
rejoices as more and more is learned through sonar, radar, quasars, lasers, about the universe he has created;
yearns for persons to learn more and more about living wholesomely, together, in this universe by following the commandments:
no murder,
no adultery,
no thievery,
no lying,
no coveting.
Come, let us worship God, and to him let us pray.

O God,
you comprehend with ease our most intricate inventions:
Patiently continue to assist us, young and old alike, more fully to understand the most intricate creation of the universe—persons themselves.
Open afresh to us this day your holy word in Scripture and fix our attention anew on Jesus, that young person through whom you revealed to us our nature and your redeeming purposes.
And, as Jesus taught disciples to pray, so we, together, lift that prayer to you:

Our Father, who art in heaven, hallowed . . .

God, whom we gather to worship,
knows the inside of pool halls as well as of country clubs,
knows the inside of union halls as well as of executive suites, and
knows you, too, inside and out.
Come, let us worship God, and to him let us pray.

O God,
you make your presence, your purposes, your power known to us in so many ways;
your earnest desire is that every person, in all the world, shall know your love through Jesus Christ; and
you commission each of us who knows you to share that knowledge in love with all persons:
Let your presence bring forth afresh our praise,
let your desire move us to faithful witnessing, so that, soon and sincerely, all persons will join us in praying to you as Jesus taught people to pray:

Our Father, who art in heaven, hallowed . . .

God, whom we gather to worship,
possesses simultaneous translation equipment far superior to that in the United Nations Assembly,
knows vastly more than the information contained in all the books cataloged by the Library of Congress, and
understands you more completely than the most able psychiatrist.
Come, let us worship God, and to him let us pray.

O God,
here we are:
some present out of habit;
some present under duress;
some present with eager expectancy;
some present in profound gratitude;
some present, not quite knowing why.
Bless each of us:
let the music inspire and refresh,
let the Creed confirm rather than confuse,
let the Scripture enlighten and direct,
let the offering excite and release,
let our prayers, silent and individual, audible and collective, be as comprehensive and as personal as the prayer Jesus gave disciples:

Our Father, who art in heaven, hallowed . . .

God, whom we gather to worship,
designed insect pollenization of plants, long before persons developed the science of fertilization;
designed the cycle of saltwater-to-atmosphere-to-rainfall, long before persons developed the science of desalinization;
designed endocrine glands and the autonomic nervous system, long before persons developed the science of chemotherapy; also
demonstrated salvation by grace through faith, long before persons developed the science of psychiatry.
Come, let us worship God, and to him let us pray.

O God,
you created human beings and directed them to subdue the earth and have dominion;
you rejoice in the discoveries persons make toward constructive management of material things:
Give us each insight this morning into your design for wholesome interpersonal relationships
between ourselves and other persons,
between ourselves and you.
Let us ponder anew and be enlightened afresh by the interpersonal relationships affirmed in the prayer Jesus taught his disciples to pray for themselves and for others:

Our Father, who art in heaven, hallowed . . .

God, whom we gather to worship,
possesses no safe retreat from the strains and stresses of human society, nor does he desire such.
He knows the anxiety of the court room, the anguish of prison, and the brutality of the firing squad, and
he knows you in your role as persecuted and as persecutor.
Come, let us worship God, and to him let us pray.

O God,
resist our efforts to deny your presence and involvement in current problems in human society.
This day let the good news of the incarnation of Jesus stab us awake to your very presence among us in our daily rounds.
Keep us from praying, "Lord, come to us," as though you were absent from us.
Let us remember anew the words of Jesus:
"Inasmuch as ye did it not to one of the least of these, ye did it not to me."
With careful attention and deep earnestness, we pray to you as Jesus taught disciples to pray:

Our Father, who art in heaven, hallowed . . .

God, whom we gather to worship,
designed the protons, neutrons, electrons, and directed their association to form nuclei, atoms, molecules, structures, and organisms.
He marks each person with unique fingerprints and yet designed human beings as social creatures.
He knows you as an individual, seeks to surround you with a loving, forgiving, supporting, and challenging fellowship of his people.
Come, let us worship God, and to him let us pray.

O God,
in the crush of traffic, the push and shove of shopping, the surge in corridors of school, we often wonder if we are known by you, or by anyone else.
In the isolation of apartments, the solitude of speeding automobiles, the seclusion of a nursing home bed, we often wonder if we are remembered by you, or by anyone else.
Remind us anew, this day, O God, that you have the whole wide world in your hands.
Assure us, once more, that you know us, each one by name and by need.
Let us never feel forsaken, nor believe that multitudes are outside your providence.
Here and now, with fresh courage and full assurance, we call you Father, and together pray to you as Jesus taught disciples to pray:

Our Father, who art in heaven, hallowed . . .

God, whom we gather to worship,
created the universe out of nothing,
declared his creation good, and
entrusted the tending of the earth to human beings.
He continues his marvelous works of creation and providence, and offers to touch, directly, the life of each person in forgiveness, regeneration, and sustaining love.
In short, God made you,
God loves you,
God commissions you, and
God holds you accountable for your individual stewardship.
Come, let us worship God, and to him let us pray.

O God,
your genius is evident in the amazing forces of gravity,
in the intricacies of life, and
in the beauty of nature;
your righteousness is evident
in the equity of moral principles,
in the redemptive purpose of your judgment, and
in the faithfulness of your promises; and
your love has been fully demonstrated, on earth, through Jesus:
We worship you, we praise you, we honor and glorify you.
Through Jesus we know you as personal and compassionate.
Therefore, with confidence and concern we pray to you as Jesus taught disciples to pray, for themselves and for others:

Our Father, who art in heaven, hallowed . . .

God, whom we gather to worship,
reveals his genius
in the creation of caterpillars which metamorphose into butterflies,
in his creation of atoms which attract and repel,
in his creation of water which rises from the oceans, distills, and falls as snow in mountains, and runs down, nourishingly, as rivers.
He reveals his power and judgment through moral laws, universally applicable and timelessly true.
He reveals his love through the incarnation of Jesus and by the fruit-bearing presence of the Holy Spirit.
Come, let us worship God, and to him let us pray.

O God,
great beyond our imagining,
wise beyond our understanding,
powerful beyond our measuring, and
loving beyond our deserving: PRAISE BE TO YOU!
Out of the abundance of your manifold grace, minister to each of us in our particular needs:
help the fortunate in their rejoicing,
comfort the grieving in their sorrow,
energize the vigorous in their achieving,
deliver the tempted in their trials,
refresh the weary in their labors,
encourage the generous in their liberality,
save the lost from their sinning.
And as you have revealed yourself as Father of our Lord Jesus, so together we pray to you:

Our Father, who art in heaven, hallowed . . .

Grace to you and peace, from God the Father, and from our Lord Jesus Christ.
God, whom we gather to worship,
is keenly interested in the outcome of the election in this city.
Are you?
He has profound concern for the welfare of Southeast Asians and for GI's.
Do you?
He knows you well, loves you deeply, is able to help you abundantly.
Are you receiving his help?
Let us worship God, and to him let us pray.

O God,
how great you are!
Sovereign over all time and space and energy;
lover of every person, desiring from each a responding love;
patient and powerful, beyond all things, yet present with us here:
WE WORSHIP YOU!
Acknowledging both your greatness and your personal interest in each of us, together we pray to you as Jesus taught disciples to pray:

Our Father, who art in heaven, hallowed . . .

God, whom we gather to worship,
knows you by name and says to you, "Good morning, Herbert and Welborn; Enid and Bertha; Dan and Beulah; Don and Lucille; Robert and Helen; Margaret, JoeAn, Marylynn, Judy, Shirley, and Patti; Harry, Tommy, Craig, Jeff, Charles, Chris, and James . . ."
He knows your needs and offers you his gifts:
forgiveness, for the penitent;
joy, for the rejoicing;
courage, for the downhearted;
comfort, for the sorrowing;
mercy, for the sinner;
wisdom, for the perplexed; and
LOVE, LOVE, REFRESHING LOVE, for each one of us!
In God's name: WELCOME!!!
Come, let us worship God, and to him let us pray.

O God,
you have marked each of us with distinguishing fingerprints,
you have entrusted each of us with special talents,
you have particular hopes and promises for us, one by one:
We are profoundly grateful
that we live in a world you have made,
in a time when you are in control,
among friends you have provided us through Jesus, our Savior.
We rejoice to lift to you our adoration and our requests, for ourselves and for others, as Jesus taught disciples to pray to you:

Our Father, who art in heaven, hallowed . . .

God, whom we gather to worship,
has given us a parable from the space age:
John Young and his partner, Charlie Duke, yonder on the moon, are "wired for sound" to persons in Houston:
heartbeat, respiration, and voice;
their lunar actions visible on television screens at Mission Control.
They have a "program of work" to be accomplished which they elect to follow and which is subject to modification.
So sensitive is this monitoring that when Young, in excitement, works too rapidly, the telemetry of his vital processes brings from Mission Control the admonition, "Slow down, John . . ."
Even so, for centuries, God has each person he has created under even more comprehensive observation:
monitoring vital signs,
counseling concerning scheduled work,
immediately available to help solve unexpected problems.
PRAISES BE TO OUR MARVELOUS GOD!!! To him let us pray.

Almighty God, creator of the universe and its sustainer,
in gracious love you sent Jesus on a glorious mission to earth, and
you have each one of us under your omniscient surveillance:
Accept our profound gratitude and abundant praise;
fix our attention on your plans for our work;
counsel us when the unexpected happens;
keep us mindful of the great crowd of witnesses watching our performance, hopeful and confident.
To you, whose concern reaches out to every person on the globe, we pray as Jesus taught disciples to pray, for themselves and for others:

Our Father, who art in heaven, hallowed . . .

God, whom we gather to worship,
rejoices that you are here amid this company of his people.
Before you is a cross, reminding you of God's suffering, serving love for you.
Before you is a baptismal font, reminding you of his forgiveness and of his ability to give new lives for old.
Before you is a Bible, reminding you of his promises and of his commands, and of his past actions for his people.
Before you is a table, reminding you of God's own presence with his people in fellowship and love.
Come, let us worship God, and to him let us pray.

O God,
you always keep watch over mankind collectively, and
you know each of us with our particular joys and sorrows:
We worship you, we adore you, we praise you!
Assist us each to receive your love and your discipline.
Refresh us, one and all, with unexpected—and unmerited—mercies.
Startle us, everyone, with new commands for our obedience for this very day, for this very week.
Because we know you through Jesus as personal, powerful, and purposeful, we are bold to pray to you, together, as Jesus taught disciples:

Our Father, who art in heaven, hallowed . . .

God bids you welcome to this special hour.
He is eager to celebrate with you your victories:
a breakthrough in loving communications with your family,
an important task well done at plant or office, store or school,
a temptation to evil resisted, a deed of kindness graciously done.
He is ready to counsel with you in your perplexities:
how best to use the precious time of summer,
how business can be conducted with compassion as well as with profit,
how nations can live constructively together in the neighborhood that this planet has become.
He is here to enfold you in his love:
to lift your shame and guilt by his forgiveness and mercy,
to call and commission you to daily deeds of eternal value,
to surprise you with joy.
Come, let us worship God, and to him let us pray.

O God,
in Jesus Christ and by the Holy Spirit you are closer to us than hands or feet, nearer to us than breathing;
you patiently labor, through persons such as we, for health and wholesomeness, justice and mercy, food adequate, clothing ample, and shelter sufficient, for all your people; and
you add to our own fumbling performance your own deeds of love:
We worship and adore you, we bless and praise you.
Work your miracles among us this day—
reward our seeking, meet our manifold needs,
commission us anew for high and holy endeavors.
And to you we pray together, for ourselves and for others, as Jesus taught disciples to address you in prayer:

Our Father, who art in heaven, hallowed . . .

God says a hearty "Thank you!" to each of you who has helped him this past week in his ministry of love and service to persons in need;
says a hearty "Well done!" to each of you who has achieved a goal which he has set before you;
says a stout "Watch out!" to any one of you toying fitfully with any temptation to sin; and
says a sure word of forgiveness to any one of you here today who confesses sin and earnestly wants pardon and regeneration through Jesus.
Yes, God is present to do great things with you—with your mind, with your heart, with your will.
Come, let us worship God, and to him let us pray.

O God,
you invite us to be fellow laborers with you,
tending the earth and ministering to all persons;
your rod and staff are used to keep us in the paths of righteousness, and to comfort us in the valley of the shadows of death:
Receive, now, our praise for your marvelous love and gracious providences.
Speak to us, afresh, your words of comfort, counsel, and command, and bind us together in a beloved and joyful fellowship of your people.
To you we pray together, for ourselves and for others, as Jesus taught disciples:

Our Father, who art in heaven, hallowed . . .

Rest assured:
God, whom we gather to worship,
is interested in the quality of relations between the United States of America and the People's Republic of China,
is interested in the quality of water in Corpus Christi Bay, and
is interested in the quality of the atmosphere with which you surround your psyche.
Righteousness, justice, and peace are his desire for nations.
Beauty, utility, and fruitfulness are his desire for natural resources.
Radiance, love, and salvation are his desire for you.
Come, let us worship God, and to him let us pray:

Our Father, who art in heaven, hallowed . . .

Greetings to you from the Lord God Almighty, maker of heaven and earth.
We are gathered here today to worship him.
To him we present our anxiety and hope
regarding plans for integration in the public school system;
regarding our excitement and concern over the establishment of an upper-level college in this community;
our plans for "change of pace" during the summer months; and
our eagerness to hear afresh God's word of
forgiveness,
direction,
encouragement, and rebuke.
Come, let us worship God, and to him let us pray.

O God,
gracious beyond our deserving,
loving beyond our imagining,
patient beyond all reason,
minister tenderly to each child of yours present here today.
Deepen the faith and trust of those who doubt.
Receive the joy and gratitude of all who rejoice.
Encourage all whose zeal for your kingdom is wavering.
Convert anyone who is in open rebellion against you.
With earnestness and confidence we lift before you the prayer Jesus taught disciples to pray, for themselves and for others:

Our Father, who art in heaven, hallowed . . .

God, whom we gather to worship,
is invisible—as are the impulses of radio and television transmission—yet nonetheless real, whether or not we know how to use abilities to transform the manifestation of his presence to suit our auditory range, our visual capacity, our cerebral processes.
God, whom we gather to worship,
upholds moral principles of justice, righteousness, and love —as pervasive and powerful and constant as the principles of
the magnetism between masses,
the genetic code in biological reproduction.
God, whom we gather to worship,
continues active within the universe of his design and creation;
continues sovereign over the affairs of individuals and of nations;
continues to approach you, personally, with the gifts of salvation, commission for service, and assurance of eternal worth and fellowship.
Come, let us worship God, and to him let us pray.

O God,
your concern embraces clean lives and clean air,
your purposes include wholesome family relationships and wholesome spiritual environment:
Be present, here and now, to give each of us startling and reassuring insight into reality.
Move us each *from* indifference *to* deep commitment to your purposes.
Move us *from* uncertainty *to* assurance that your will shall prevail.
Move us *from* self-justification *to* acknowledgment of your standards of value.
Capture our minds and our hearts and our wills, in order that we may earnestly and effectively offer to you the prayer Jesus gave disciples:

Our Father, who art in heaven, hallowed . . .

God, whom we gather to worship,
thundered his word and will to Moses at Mt. Sinai,
whispered his word and will to Elijah at Mt. Horeb,
acted out his word and will in Jesus from Bethlehem to Calvary and in the resurrection.
He still imparts his word and will today to persons such as you and me through the Bible, made true and lively and relevant by the Holy Spirit.
Come, let us worship God, and to him let us pray.

O God,
you have fashioned beauty in your created universe,
you have demonstrated your goodness throughout the centuries, and
you have led persons to truth:
We worship you! We praise you!
Assist each of us today, more and more,
to enjoy the beauty with which you have surrounded us;
to spread abroad, in our words and deeds, goodness like unto yours; and
to do the truth as we have found it in your commands and promises.
And now, reminded of our special needs and of all the world's ills, we pray to you, together, as Jesus taught disciples to pray:

Our Father, who art in heaven, hallowed . . .

God, whom we gather to worship,
swung the galaxies into space and formed the universe,
drew into gravitational harmony this solar system,
provided in the orbits of earth and moon seasons and tides,
brought forth on earth life, in plant and fish and fowl and human beings, and
sent Jesus to demonstrate to persons how to live abundantly in his good creation.
Come, let us worship God, and to him let us pray.

O God,
we expect to meet you here and now
in bread and drink,
by word, written and spoken,
through your people present with us, and
as the Holy Spirit among us:
Receive our adoration for your power and wisdom,
our gratitude for your glorious creation,
our response of trust and obedience to your mercy and love.
Bind us together anew as a loving, forgiving, rejoicing company of disciples of Jesus, and
commission us each afresh to be channels of your mercy to all other persons.
To you we pray together, with mind and voice and heart uniting, the prayer Jesus gave as a pattern:

Our Father, who art in heaven, hallowed . . .

God, whom we gather to worship,
witnesses the frenzy of spectators at football games;
hears cheers, organized and massive; and
is aware of the partisanship of those assembled.
When is the last time you *gave a lusty cheer for God?*
Come, let us worship God, and to him let us pray.

O God,
the doer of all things good,
the worker of miracles in the contest of life,
help us today to sing "Amens" for what they are—loud "So Let It Be's";
help us today to affirm with vigor our "Hallelujahs!"—"Praise the Lord!"
Fix our eyes, in eager anticipation, upon Jesus, "the pioneer and perfecter of our faith," who taught disciples to participate with zest, and to pray with zeal and expectancy:

Our Father, who art in heaven, hallowed . . .

We are gathered to worship God . . .
with minds and hearts set on many things:
joy and sadness,
faith and doubt,
guilt and forgiveness,
private concerns and social problems,
severe temptations and gloriously constructive opportunities.
God bids you a cordial welcome, and promises to meet you helpfully at the point of your most pressing need.
Come, let us worship God, and to him let us pray.

O God,
in wisdom you have made us, in mercy you sustain us, and in love you reach out to help each one of us:
Rejoice with those who rejoice,
and weep with those who weep;
meet our faith with good gifts,
and our doubt with renewed trust;
forgive our sin confessed,
and cleanse our minds and hearts with new love;
deliver us from yielding to demeaning temptations,
and direct us in using our opportunities for service.
To you we join our voices and hearts in the prayer Jesus gave disciples to pray, for themselves and for others:

Our Father, who art in heaven, hallowed . . .

God, whom we gather to worship,
took gregarious carbon,
sturdy iron,
precious gold,
fluctuating mercury,
volatile phosphorous,
scarce argon,
nurturing nitrogen,
and a host of other amazingly diverse elements, and formed with them an astoundingly beautiful, fruitful, and enduring universe.
Come, let us worship God, and to him let us pray.

O God,
skillful beyond our imagining,
facile beyond our equaling,
help us become vitally alive to your genius.
Deepen our appreciation for the infinitely wide variety of persons you have placed upon this planet.
Assist us each to perform more skillfully the special functions for which you have made us.
Help all human beings, through Jesus, to learn to pray to you with earnestness and anticipation:

Our Father, who art in heaven, hallowed . . .

God, whom we gather to worship,
took the offerings of Alexander Graham Bell and Guglielmo Marconi and bound humankind in a network of voice-to-ear communication;
took the offerings of Orville and Wilbur Wright and bound humankind in a globe-encircling pattern of transportation.
He can take your daily offerings of labor also and use them in blessing an ever-widening company of his people.
Come, let us worship God, and to him let us pray.

O God,
by your creative word the universe came into being, and
by your continuing providence humankind continues to enlarge dominion within it:
Keep each of us conscious of our particular responsibilities and opportunities to be channels of your blessings to others.
Let our words, our acts, our lives be useful to you in your unceasing efforts to achieve wholesome living for every person.
To this end we pray together as Jesus taught disciples:

Our Father, who art in heaven, hallowed . . .

God, whom we gather to worship,
is acquainted with the congestion of commuter freeways, morning and evening;
has knowledge of crowded airports, crammed bus terminals, stacked-up elevator shafts;
observes jostling shoppers and crushing stadium exits.
His amazing love reaches out to each person in such mobs, and his heart calls each person by name:
Ruel and Anna; Sarah and Benjamin; Gretchen and Hans; Ivan and Olga; Pierre and Colette; Isabella and Juan; Giuseppe and Rosa; Tom and Mary . . .
Come, let us worship God, and to him let us pray.

O God,
you see us each almost engulfed in the sea of humanity, and you understand our fear of anonymity:
Refresh us this day by calling us each by name.
Let us take new courage before we plunge, once again, into our daily affairs—
courage to live as responsible individuals because our particular words and deeds register with you, for approval or for correction,
courage to see all other persons as our brothers and sisters by your appointment,
courage to pray, for ourselves and for others, as Jesus taught disciples to pray:

Our Father, who art in heaven, hallowed . . .

God, whom we gather to worship,
made us so that the blood of a pauper or of a patrician can be transfused to save the life of a child or of an adult;
guided persons in developing techniques for drawing, storing, matching blood from willing donors; and
rejoices in the lifesaving infusion of blood into traumatized persons.
Come, let us worship God, and to him let us pray.

O God,
receive our gratitude for the miracle of blood—
nourishingly coursing through our bodies,
generously given for another's need,
marvelously stored to meet widespread catastrophe.
Fix our attention anew on the lifesaving miracle of Jesus' blood, sacrificially given for human salvation.
Infuse into each of us this day that spiritual quality of his life which, bathing every cell of our body, enables us to respond to you in love and obedience.
Make us "blood brothers and sisters" in your redeemed and redeeming family, and cause us to pray to you, together, as Jesus taught disciples to pray:

Our Father, who art in heaven, hallowed . . .

God, whom we gather to worship,
knew harmony before Palestrina,
electricity before Leyden,
sculpture before Michelangelo,
relativity before Einstein.
He knows what is yet ahead for humankind.
Come, let us worship God, and to him let us pray.

O God,
knowledgeable beyond our imagining, our praise goes forth to you.
Our gratitude increases because your love for us as persons is as vast as your knowledge, and your helpful Presence enfolds each one of us.
Stimulate our minds to discover even more treasures you have for us within your universe.
Quicken our hearts to love more expansively and constructively each person about us.
Enrich us with deepening awareness of your gift-giving Spirit, from whom we can never escape.
To you, the Father Almighty, maker of heaven and earth, we pray together as Jesus taught disciples to pray:

Our Father, who art in heaven, hallowed . . .

God, whom we gather to worship,
calls some of his disciples to live in lands dictators rule;
some, to live in realms over which kings have sovereignty;
some, to live in close-knit communities of clans;
some, to live in nations where the people have achieved self-government under constitutional law.
Yet over all such systems he exercises ultimate governance.
Come, let us worship God, and to him let us pray.

O God,
you have caused our lives to be lived within the United States of America, and
you have seen this political experiment celebrate the two-hundredth anniversary of its founding:
Let our gratitude for this privilege be more and more expressed to you through rightful citizenship in this particular form of human government:
by participation in party precinct meetings—with integrity,
by proper contributions to campaigns of competent candidates,
by insightful correspondence with members of Congress and legislatures,
by constructive monitoring of actions of city and county officials,
by informed following of matters of national policy,
by conversation and conduct affirming "this nation, under God."
And mindful of others of your children called to live under other forms of human government, we more earnestly pray as Jesus taught disciples to pray:

Our Father, who art in heaven, hallowed . . .

God, whom we gather to worship,
brushes the forests in the fall with brilliant colors;
spangles the white beaches with fascinating shells;
sails across the skies clouds in endless variety; and
peoples the streets of every community with precious persons, intriguing and different.
Come, let us worship God, and to him let us pray.

O God, great Creator,
heighten today our sensitivity to the splendors with which you endow your universe, and
deepen our awareness of one another.
Give us fresh appreciation for the richness given humankind because of varying skin colors and racial heritage.
Give us renewed attention to the captivating variety of persons washed beside us by the tides of communal living.
Give us keener anticipation of the blessings awaiting us from the cultural diversity that is like the atmosphere caressing the globe.
Praise be to you, O God, Creator Supreme. As you have taught us, through Jesus, we also pray:

Our Father, who art in heaven, hallowed . . .

Do not believe that
God, whom we gather to worship,
misses out on the excitement of county and state fairs:
the entering of handiwork for judging,
the showing of livestock for grading,
the renewing of acquaintances,
the "doing" of the midway,
the inspecting of new products.
Come, let us worship God, and to him let us pray.

O God,
you have commissioned us to labor, and
you appreciate work diligently and well done:
Receive our grateful thanks
for the productivity of the land,
for the creations of the kitchen,
for the garments from sewing machines,
for the joys of wholesome human fellowship.
Keep us mindful of the benefactions
of leisure as well as of labor,
of giving as well as of growing,
of compassion as well as of cheering.
And for ourselves and for others we pray to you, together,
as Jesus taught disciples to pray:

Our Father, who art in heaven, hallowed . . .

Rest assured:
God, whom we gather to worship,
knows it all:
a b c d e f g . . . aleph, beth, gimel, daleth . . . alpha, beta, gamma, delta . . . or however the letters of a language go;
5 × 5, 9 × 8, 6 × 4 . . . the square root of 625 . . . the area of a circle;
the speed of light . . . the chemical composition of vitamins . . . the date and significance of the Battle of Hastings.
He also knows:
the power of love to dissolve hate,
the alchemy of forgiveness and restoration,
the priceless worth of Christlike integrity,
the esoteric ministries of the Holy Spirit.
Come, let us worship God, and to him let us pray.

O God,
your constancy and revelations spark human beings to learning and education:
Guide us as a community of your people within the larger community of this city, so that we may bear faithful and telling witness
that public education without Christ-given foundations and dimensions is like building sand castles on a tide-swept beach.
To this end we more frevently pray as Jesus taught disciples to pray:

Our Father, who art in heaven, hallowed . . .

God, whom we gather to worship,
brings forth from the somber soil a radiant array of spring flowers;
emblazons the sky with the arch of seven glorious hues;
colors the birds' plumage with a myriad of varied tints.
It is he whose artistry we celebrate.
Come, let us worship God, and to him let us pray.

O God, our Father,
we praise you for the splendor of the flowers!
We praise you for the glory of the rainbows!
We praise you for the beauty of flying creatures!
Encourage each of us to celebrate also your artistry in the varied skin tones you have given us human beings:
pink and brown, red and black,
yellow and the various shades in between.
Acknowledging the creaturely status all of us have within the universe, we pray to you, for ourselves and for all others, as Jesus taught disciples to pray:

Our Father, who art in heaven, hallowed . . .

God, whom we gather to worship,
knows the masks we so often wear:
tolerance, when we feel hate;
acceptance, when we feel disdain;
calmness, when storms rage within;
friendliness, when we plot revenge;
sympathy, when we are jealous.
Praise to God for his continuing love for us—sinners that we are!
Praise to God for his continuing acceptance of us—even when we disfigure his image in which we are created!
Praise to God for continuing to dispatch the Holy Spirit, who can work miracles of plastic surgery on our contorted countenances.
Come, let us worship God, and to him let us pray.

O God, our Father,
you look upon us for what we can become, by your grace; rather than for what we are, by our sin;
you have molded us in the first place, and can, even now, remold us as clay on a potter's wheel:
Gently rework, here and now, the deep wells of our emotions, so that love, trust, joy, and forgiving mercy will light up our countenances.
Having been blest by you this day, teach us to sing with the psalmist: "Hope in God . . . , who is the health of my countenance, and my God."
And to you, with thanksgiving, we pray:

Our Father, who art in heaven, hallowed . . .

God, whom we gather to worship,
has seen people, upon the physical death of their friends,
expose the bodies to the sun and carrion birds, or
deposit the bodies in soil or catacombs, or
mummify the bodies in arid climates, or
burn the bodies beside sacred rivers, or
place the bodies in medical school laboratories;
has seen people, upon the physical death of their friends,
greet the event with unrelieved wailing and anguish, or
with the celebration of a wake, or
with stoic resignation, or
with joyful assurance of resurrection.
Come, let us worship God, and to him let us pray.

O God, our Father,
we praise you for your marvelous design of the human body,
and for the glorious environment of your creation for the living of human existence—the earth;
we give you grateful thanks for the earthly life of Jesus,
in which we have clear example for wholesome human, earthly living.
We rejoice in your glorious resurrection of Jesus
from the tomb, and
for your assurance that your people, also,
will find physical death an amazing transition
rather than an unrelieved tragedy.
Help us prepare to pray, at the time of our physical demise,
Jesus' prayer at such a time in his life:
"Father, into thy hands I commend my spirit."
And for our living now, as many days as your providence provides, we pray together another prayer Jesus used:

Our Father, who art in heaven, hallowed . . .

God, whom we gather to worship,
is interested, to be sure, in the Cowboys and Oilers, the Dolphins and Patriots, the Lions and Bears, the Packers and Steelers . . . and also in the Yankees and Royals, the Reds and the Phillies.
He knows about the Sooners, the Crimson Tide, the Nittany Lions, the Tar Heels, the Cornhuskers, the Fighting Irish, the Trojans.
But rest assured, he is more interested in
honesty in business dealings,
righteousness in political affairs,
justice and mercy in legal proceedings,
integrity in personal relationships, and
compassionate acts for all the world's neglected.
Come, let us worship God, and to him let us pray.

O God, our Father,
you have placed us in a time of one thousand and one distractions, and
your providence oversees all aspects of human activity:
We bless and praise you for the precious and precarious freedom of choices.
Stimulate us to choose to follow with enthusiasm and consecrated diligence the triumphs
of good over evil,
of righteousness over injustice,
of love over hate,
of integrity over dissembling,
of honesty over deceit,
of care over neglect.
To the end that your will shall be done, on earth,
in every aspect of human activity,
we earnestly pray, for ourselves and for others,
the prayer Jesus gave disciples:

Our Father, who art in heaven, hallowed . . .

God, whom we gather to worship,
knows intimately the burdens persons bear:
their own personal ailments: physical, mental, emotional;
pain and distress over the unhealthy condition of loved ones;
the tensions and anxieties arising in employment, or the lack of it;
the perplexities of retirement;
the concerns about injustice, irresponsibility, lostness, affecting unknown multitudes.
God is eagerly ready to minister helpfully to you—and through you—this day.
Come, let us worship God, and to him let us pray.

O God, our Father,
you forgive sin confessed and repented of, and can bring healing to spirits depressed by sin;
you can give physical and emotional healing, or supply the strength to bear such ailments;
you move in mercy to others whom we lift up to you in prayer;
you supply wisdom to those who seek it from you; and
you channel much of your grace for the needs of the world through willing persons such as we:
We praise you for all your blessings to us in the past;
we praise you for your unceasing labors for good among all persons;
we thank you for the powerful presence of the Holy Spirit, active among us here and now.
Graciously minister to our particular needs, and to the needs of those we remember before you; and
sensitize and activate each of us as channels of your blessed love to others as we pray the prayer Jesus gave disciples:

Our Father, who art in heaven, hallowed . . .

God, whom we gather to worship,
spangles the night sky with myriads of stars;
bathes the planet earth by day with energy-packed rays from the sun, so brilliant that all other stars disappear;
also illumines the minds of human beings with knowledge and understanding; and
beams upon the people of the earth the quintessence of wisdom and saving knowledge through Jesus.
Come, let us worship God, and to him let us pray.

O God, our Father,
within your vast creation we are infinitessimal specks, and yet by your providence we probe the farthest reaches of the universe and penetrate the secrets of molecules, atoms, neutrons, and nuclei:
We praise you for all that you help us to understand about matter, about energy, about physical life.
We praise you more for your ceaseless activity in helping us to know you better, and to understand more precisely your purposes for us, creatures made in your image and likeness.
Let the spectacular radiance of your revelation in Jesus cause us to flourish in the achievements for which you made us.
And to that end we pray to you again the prayer Jesus gave disciples to pray, for themselves and for others:

Our Father, who art in heaven, hallowed . . .

God, whom we gather to worship,
observes intently as human beings probe the surface of Mars by Viking satellites;
rejoices in the amazing teamwork, astonishing technical skill, persistent patience manifested in such endeavor; and
is gratified by the continuing zeal of human beings to discover more and more of the treasures he has built into the universe designed for their habitat.
Come, let us worship God, and to him let us pray.

O God, our Father,
your intelligence conceived,
your word created,
your power sustains,
the universe in all its vastness and intricacy;
your steady laws,
your faithful elements,
your grand design,
makes possible advance in understanding the universe by human beings:
We praise you for magnificent achievements.
Grant that with fascination and with commitment of vast resources human beings will also give continuing and effective attention to discovering upon this planet
avenues to peace, highways to justice, boulevards to foodstuffs, channels of righteousness, and the atmosphere conducive to wholesome living for all.
With "Hallelujahs!" and with earnest pleading we pray together as Jesus taught his disciples to pray:

Our Father, who art in heaven, hallowed . . .

God, whom we gather to worship,
continually works miracles.
He formed the universe by the power of his word, and sustains it through his wisdom and grace,
He delivered his people from bondage in Egypt and restored them from exile.
He raised up prophets to speak his word, and priests to minister his mercies.
He sent Jesus in love to reclaim the lost and preserves in Scripture the record of his saving actions.
Among us he works miracles day by day:
the lost are *saved,*
the sick are *healed,*
the inquiring are *enlightened,*
the sorrowful are *comforted*
the adventuring are *guided,*
the willing are *Spirit-filled.*
Come, let us worship God, and to him let us pray.

O God, our Father,
we praise you for your mighty acts of yesteryears.
Stab us awake to your present-day miracles in and among us:
our willingness to forgive and to be forgiven,
our ability to love and to receive reclaiming love,
our privilege to hear you and speak to you in prayer,
our capacity to be infilled by the Holy Spirit.
Help us to celebrate with one another your contemporary miracles among us, telling our stories, giving you the praise.
And, that every person may come to know the glories of your miraculous working in their lives, we pray to you as Jesus taught disciples to pray:

Our Father, who art in heaven, hallowed . . .

God, whom we gather to worship,
watched over the Pilgrims as they composed the Mayflower Compact, over the representatives gathered in Philadelphia as they signed the Declaration of Independence.
He wept with the Cherokees as they plodded on their trail of tears.
He hurt as brother battled brother from Gettysburg to Appomattox.
He observed with interest as the golden spike united railroad tracks joining the nation together from sea to shining sea, and
he seeks to work constructively with citizens pursuing the goals of liberty and justice for all.
Come, let us worship God, and to him let us pray.

O God, our Father,
you called Abraham to become a pilgrim, seeking a city that has foundations, whose builder and maker you are;
you scattered the disciples of Jesus to carry the good news of your redemptive participation with humankind toward wholesome living for all:
Keep us ever obedient to our commission, as your people,
both to build a society for the blessing of all and
to spread abroad the glorious gospel of your saving involvement in the life and labors of persons all around the globe.
Mindful of the preciousness of daily bread,
of our continuing need to be forgiven and to forgive, and
of your ultimate sovereignty,
we earnestly pray, for ourselves and for others, as Jesus taught disciples to pray:

Our Father, who art in heaven, hallowed . . .

God, whom we gather to worship,
is imagined by many to be
only the Preparer—not a Participant in his universe;
only an Executioner—not a Probation Officer for offenders;
only a Life Force—not a Living Presence throughout creation;
only a Demander—not a Supplier for his people;
only a Frightening Mystery—not a Familiar Friend.
Ceaselessly God endeavors to reveal himself to people, so as to remove from them dread, superstition, disdain, illusion.
Come, let us worship God, and to him let us pray.

O God, our Father,
you sent your Son Jesus to earth to become a living demonstration of your self-giving love;
you are eager and able to shepherd your people in the paths of righteousness, beside still waters, and safely through the valley of the shadows;
you pour forth from the windows of heaven boundless mercies and blessings upon your trusting people;
you control the universe in its intricacies and vastness, but intimately abide with persons who welcome you:
We sing for joy that, through Jesus, we have come to know you as our gracious, loving heavenly Father.
Out of such glorious experience, and with confirmed confidence, we pray to you, for ourselves and for others, as Jesus taught disciples:

Our Father, who art in heaven, hallowed . . .

God, whom we gather to worship,
gives us freely and regularly oxygen to breathe;
gives us the rhythm of day and night for work and for rest;
gives us the bounty of farmland and orchards, rivers and oceans, for food;
gives us the energy of the sun and the treasures of the earth for industry.
He also gives us the record of his self-revelation in the Scripture,
the demonstration of his nature and will in Jesus,
the glorious blessings of the Holy Spirit's graces and gifts.
Come, let us worship God, and to him let us pray.

O God, our Father,
your gifts are new every morning and fresh every evening,
your blessings nourish and sustain us and guide us in wholesome living:
We praise you for your gifts and honor you for your mercies.
As we receive in thanksgiving, enable us also to become agents of your gifts and mercies to others,
so they, like us, shall come to know and love and trust you, and
shall learn to pray with earnestness and joy
as Jesus taught disciples to address you in prayer:

Our Father, who art in heaven, hallowed . . .

God, whom we gather to worship,
knows how salt air eats away at stout metal,
how acid effluents penetrate aquatic creatures,
how sulphuric fumes choke life from flying birds;
also knows how hate corrodes a sweet spirit,
jealousy penetrates a delicate psyche,
pride chokes a tender conscience.
Come, let us worship God, and to him let us pray.

O God, our Father,
we thank you for inspiring human beings to discover and apply
antirust paint to seaside metal,
antiacids to neutralize effluents,
antismog devices for industrial discharges.
We honor and praise you for all the antidotes you supply for making our passage through life less and less contaminating:
love and forgiveness to counteract hate,
widespread gifts and mercies to counteract jealousy,
wholesome humility to counteract pride.
Keep us ever mindful of corrosive forces impinging upon us, and
of sweet discharges our lives can give
off to bless the human environment.
As we think of harvests for food and of blessed human relationships the world around, and of your sovereign providence over all, we pray to you, together, as Jesus taught disciples to pray:

Our Father, who art in heaven, hallowed . . .

PRAYERS FOR SPECIAL DAYS AND OCCASIONS

NEW YEAR

God, whom we gather to worship,
inventories his universe as carefully as merchants inventory their businesses;
gives bountifully, without regard to Internal Revenue regulations; and
loves you with affection, skill, and generous grace.
Come, let us worship God, and to him let us pray.

O God,
generous and gracious, you neither slumber nor sleep, and though timeless, you give us a sense of time:
Here we stand at the close of another year as the earth completes its swing about the sun.
We mark its close with gratitude to you,
with appreciation for one another, and
with new resolution for faithful obedience to you in our service to other persons.
We acknowledge your amazing "splashdown" on earth in Bethlehem through Jesus, and your promise, faithfully fulfilled, to dwell with each of us through the living, energizing Holy Spirit.
How silently, how silently the wondrous gift is given.
So do you impart to human hearts the blessings of your heaven.
No ear may hear your coming, but in this world of sin,
Where meek souls will receive him, still the dear Christ enters in.
And as he taught us, so together we pray to you:

Our Father, who art in heaven, hallowed . . .

EPIPHANY

God, whom we gather to worship,
gave Jesus, born in Bethlehem, as the fulfillment of his promise to his people, the children of Abraham;
called those persons of another tradition, the Wise Men, to seek out Jesus, and to worship him.
Yes, God, maker of heaven and earth,
so loved the world—and each person in it—
that he gave his only begotten Son
that whoever believes in him
shall not perish, but have everlasting life.
Come, let us worship God, and to him let us pray.

O God,
you reach out to each of us in Jesus to save us:
Develop within us each the radiant desire and the effective will to convince all persons we meet
of your desire and ability to give them new lives for old,
and to fit them for an eternity of love, joy, peace, and faithfulness in company with you and with all the saints.
And as Jesus taught disciples to pray to you, for themselves and for others, so we join our hearts and our voices, praying:

Our Father, who art in heaven, hallowed . . .

EASTER

Christ is risen! He is risen, indeed!
Hallelujah!
The Lord God Omnipotent reigns!
To the King, immortal, invisible, the only God,
be honor and glory, forever and ever! Amen.
Come, let us worship God, and to him let us pray.

O God,
through Jesus' sacrificial death and glorious resurrection you have caused sin to lose its sting and death its power:
We worship you,
we adore you,
we praise you, and give thanks continually.
With your blessings abounding for us, and mindful of so many persons still burdened with sin and fearful of death, we earnestly pray to you as Jesus taught disciples to pray:

Our Father, who art in heaven, hallowed . . .

THE SACRAMENTS

God, whom we gather to worship,
seeks to get your attention
by ink lettered on paper as words in the Bible,
by water applied from the baptismal font,
by common bread and simple juice set before you on this table.
He who maintains the vast universe by his wisdom and power wants you to know that he knows and loves you,
that he who gave you physical existence
rejoices in your triumphs for good,
weeps with you in your sadnesses and disappointments, and
eagerly responds to your inquiries for truth.
It is God who calls you to joyful, useful, expanding fellowship with persons present here with you in worship.
Come, let us worship God, and to him let us pray.

O God, our Father,
you have given water a holy significance,
bread a sacramental character, and
wine a eucharistic joy;
you can hallow by your presence
a jury room, a beauty parlor,
a research laboratory;
your word—in Scripture, Sacrament, and sermon—is our life:
We worship you, we bless and praise you!
But more—because of the revelation to us of your love in the incarnation of Jesus, we have from him learned to call you Father!
Now, together, we open to you our hearts and minds and wills as we pray:

Our Father, who art in heaven, hallowed . . .

COMMUNION

God, whom we gather to worship,
looks with interest at the Congress assembled in Washington, D.C.,
looks with concern at each person now in the county jail, and
looks with anticipation at each person present here preparing to join one another and their Lord and Savior at the holy table.
Come, let us worship God, and to him let us pray.

O God,
Sovereign over all, yet exercising much of your sovereignty through human beings,
let our worship of you this day remind each of us of our individual responsibilities
as citizens in this democratic republic,
as residents of this county, and
as communicants at this holy table.
We praise you for your trust in us, and
we rejoice in our assurance, through Jesus Christ, that the whole wide world is in your hands.
As Jesus taught disciples, so we, together, address you in prayer, for ourselves and for others:

Our Father, who art in heaven, hallowed . . .

GRADUATION

God, whom we gather to worship,
rejoices over those who have marked a milestone by their graduation from high school or from college,
rejoices with those who can contemplate refreshing vacations during the summer, and
causes the very bells of heaven to ring over each person who today receives his forgiving, regenerating love through Jesus.
Come, let us worship God, and to him let us pray.

O God,
minds you have given us, for learning about the world;
hands you have given us, for doing significant tasks within the world;
wills you have given us, for responding in obedience to your purposes for the world.
Come this day, again, to woo our hearts:
teach us to love ourselves as you love us;
teach us to love one another as we love ourselves, by your grace;
teach us to love you, our loving heavenly Father, best of all.
And, as Jesus taught disciples, so, together, we pray:

Our Father, who art in heaven, hallowed . . .

LOCAL FESTIVALS

God, whom we gather to worship,
takes interest in Buccaneer Days, in the Kentucky Derby, and in the New Orleans Open.
His creation in nature inspires artists, such as those exhibiting their works today in nearby South Bluff Park.
His redeeming love in Jesus prompted many of the musical masterpieces of Handel, Haydn, and Bach.
His forgiving mercies can make your life a thing of beauty and a joy forever.
Come, let us worship God, and to him let us pray.

O God,
let our worship of you this day broaden our appreciation of the zest of fellowship, the glories of your creation, and the ecstasy of rhythm and harmony.
Speak to us anew of love, of mercy, of forgiveness, and of newness of life.
Fix afresh our wills upon the teaching of Jesus, our Lord and Master, who gave disciples a pattern of prayer to lift to you:

Our Father, who art in heaven, hallowed . . .

LABOR SUNDAY

God, whom we gather to worship,
brought into being the universe by his mighty act of creation,
labors diligently within it this very day, and
calls persons to join him in useful, significant, people-serving labors.
Come, let us worship God, and to him let us pray.

O God,
you so love the world—and every person in it—as to labor constantly for humankind's salvation in and by and through Jesus;
you call each person to a high and holy vocation of labor of hand and heart, of brain and brawn:
We praise you for the fruitfulness of the soil under people's cultivation,
for the bounty of material goods produced through people's ingenuity,
for the blessing of music, art, and drama, through human response to your inspiration, and
for the hope of genuine representative government among us guided by you.
To you be glory and honor and thankfulness.
Recognizing your concern for *all* persons this day, and acknowledging our need for your present help,
we pray together as Jesus taught disciples to pray:

Our Father, who art in heaven, hallowed . . .

HUNTING SEASON

Greetings to you from the Lord God Almighty, maker of heaven and earth!
We gather here today to worship him.
To him we present our concern and hope regarding persons dear to us.
To him we present our excitement regarding opportunities before us and challenges laid upon us.
To him we present our gratitude and joy for life itself, for the beauties of creation, and for the sure and certain promises from God himself.
Come, let us worship God, and to him let us pray.

O God,
gracious beyond our deserving,
loving beyond our imagining,
patient beyond all reason,
minister tenderly to each person present here today:
Deepen the faith and trust of those who doubt;
receive the joy and gratitude of all who know your love and mercy;
encourage all whose zeal for your kingdom is wavering;
convert anyone here who is walking away from your gracious love.
(And, O God, spare the hunters and protect the hunted during deer season!)
With renewed earnestness and confidence we lift to you the prayer Jesus taught disciples to pray, for themselves and for others:

Our Father, who art in heaven, hallowed . . .

REFORMATION SUNDAY

God, whom we gather to worship,
looked with favor upon the protestants within the church generations ago: John Wycliffe, John Hus, John Calvin, Ulrich Zwingli, Martin Luther . . .
persons who protested contemporary situations because of their zeal to see radical changes in the status quo,
changes that would bring restoration of the Word of God as the fundamental determiner of the faith and practice of all human beings.
Come, let us worship God, and to him let us pray.

O God,
under whose will many have been protestants against contemporary conditions,
so lead us this day, that your Word and Spirit will give the clear specifics of any protest we raise, and
so direct us that our protests will have as their goal the fulfilling of the petitions in the prayer Jesus gave his disciples:

Our Father, who art in heaven, hallowed . . .

ALL HALLOWS' EVE

God, whom we gather to worship,
causes the hills to be a riot of color in fall splendor, and
causes human beings to rejoice in the cool, crisp, silvery light of the harvest moon.
He has seen the eve of All Saints' Day disintegrate into a night of masked prowlers and beggars known as trick-or-treaters.
Come, let us worship God, and to him let us pray.

O God, our Father,
mindful that without your self-revelation to us in Jesus we might fear spooks and goblins every night,
might wail and howl whenever a loved one physically dies, and
might worship the moon,
we gratefully open our hearts and minds to you in praise and thanksgiving, and we pray to you together the prayer Jesus gave disciples:

Our Father, who art in heaven, hallowed . . .

THANKSGIVING

God, whom we gather to worship,
caused President Lincoln to call this nation, in the midst of fratricidal strife, to a day of national thanksgiving;
caused the Congress of the United States of America to enact legislation setting aside annually such a day; and
inspired successive Presidents to issue proclamations for the observance of such days in years of peace and of war, in years of plenty and of recession, in years of harmony and of discord.
Come, let us worship God, and to him let us pray.

O God,
presider over the affairs of persons and of nations, move us to thanksgiving
not because of what we have, but because of whose we are;
not because of present blessing, but because of your continuing providence;
not because of the moment, but because of the eternity of salvation.
Let our thanksgiving be expressed
not in feasting, but in sharing;
not in passive enjoyment, but in participating service;
not in an annual act, but in daily attitude.
And because your concern for wholesome living encompasses every person upon the earth, we pray for ourselves and for others:

Our Father, who art in heaven, hallowed . . .

BIBLE SUNDAY

God, whom we gather to worship,
saw to it that there were
persons to receive his revelations and experience his providences,
to formulate alphabets and fabricate papyrus,
to remember and record his words and deeds,
to translate and distribute what was written,
so we can have before us the Holy Bible in our particular dialect.
Come, let us worship God, and to him let us pray.

O God, our Father,
we praise you for all you have done to reveal yourself to persons,
for all who are remembered and recorded in yesteryears,
for all who persevered in preserving such records.
We praise you for all you continue to do to reveal yourself,
for the Bible, now in over 1,200 dialects,
for the revealing Word lived out on earth by Jesus,
for the Holy Spirit present to make true and lively these printed words.
We praise you for all you promise yet to do for us and for all:
for the new creation, yet to come;
for life after physical death, yet to be ours;
for everlasting victory of good over evil, love over hate, peace over war.
Zealous for the completion of your redeeming, re-creating, restoring purposes, we the more earnestly pray for the whole creation as Jesus taught disciples:

Our Father, who art in heaven, hallowed . . .

CHRISTMAS

God, whom we gather to worship,
caused petroleum sources to be formed in the earth's subterranean strata;
causes rain and snow to fall in the highlands so that waters flow down through canyons and river valleys, usable to generate electricity; and
inspired Edison to persevere until the incandescent bulb glowed, enabling us to have for our enjoyment the multihued, twinkling lights that grace homes and villages and cities at Christmastime.
Come, let us worship God, and to him let us pray.

O God, our Father,
amid the gaiety, lights, exciting packages, high hopes, and heightened generosity of this Christmas season,
keep us steadily mindful
of the humble stable and its precious resident,
of humdrum Nazareth and its maturing child,
of welcoming Galilee, amazed Decapolis, hostile Jerusalem,
of hideous cross and open tomb, and
of the marvelous Savior and Lord emerging—
through whom, down through the centuries, human beings
have found light everlasting,
power sufficient, and
joy beyond equal.
As that Savior taught disciples, so we, together, lift to you with earnest, trusting hearts the prayer:

Our Father, who art in heaven, hallowed . . .

CHRISTMAS

God, whom we gather to worship,
has his eye upon the astronauts and on the longshoremen and shippers,
has his heart set on your good, and fulfills his promises to his people.
Come, let us worship God, and to him let us pray.

O God,
mighty and merciful, here we are, caught up in the swirl of Christmas:
gifts,
cards,
food,
decorations and parties.
Give us an hour of calm with you.
Here we are, tense in our relationships with one another:
with parents,
with spouses,
with children,
with employees and with customers.
Give us an hour of calm with one another.
Here we are: confused in values,
perplexed in goals,
poignant in reflection.
Give us an hour of calm with Christ, our Lord.
Let us see anew that our chief end is to glorify you:
to love you with heart and mind and soul and strength,
to love one another for your sake.
Praise to you for your mercy and patience, for your presence and your power. Catching our breath and opening our hearts, we pray to you as Jesus taught disciples to pray, for themselves and for others:

Our Father, who art in heaven, hallowed . . .

CONFESSION

CALLS TO CONFESSION
PRAYERS
GOOD NEWS

CALLS TO CONFESSION
PRAYERS

PRAYERS OF CONFESSION

CALLS TO CONFESSION, PRAYERS, GOOD NEWS

CALL TO CONFESSION

How often we see the glorious, mighty works of God only as events in the past: the exodus from Egypt, the return from exile, the coming of Jesus at Bethlehem, the triumphal entry of Jesus into Jerusalem.

How sinful is our unawareness of God's mighty works in our time and place. From such dullness, good Lord, deliver us.

CONFESSION

Silent, private.

In unison, aloud:

O God, our Father, you sent Jesus in love to claim a city and each of its citizens, for a kingdom of fellowship and service, and you saw him rejected, betrayed, deserted, condemned and crucified: We confess that all too often we do not respond, in trust and acceptance, to Jesus' redeeming approach to us. Forgive us such egregious sin. Help us to open our hearts and minds, our wills and spirits, to our approaching Sovereign, and to say in joy: "Even so, come, Lord Jesus." Amen.

GOOD NEWS OF GOD'S FORGIVING NATURE AND CLEANSING POWER

The saying is sure and worthy of full acceptance, that Christ Jesus came into the world to save sinners. Our sin we have acknowledged; our desire for forgiveness we have declared; our longing for amendment we have proclaimed. Praise God for his miracles of pardon, restoration, and strengthening in righteousness!

GLORIA PATRI

CALL TO CONFESSION

How sad to live "out of touch" with other persons. How glad Robinson Crusoe was when another person joined him. Yet how frequently we "insulate" ourselves from people. From such sinning, good Lord, deliver us.

CONFESSION

Silent, private.
In unison, aloud:

O God, our Father, you give us the marvelous gifts of compassion, sensitivity, and imagination to share the feelings of others: We acknowledge that all too often we let compassion become pity, pity become despite, despite become hostility turning us from fellowship with others. Forgive our misuse of such treasure. Enable us to move through compassion to wholesome, constructive companionship with others, for Jesus' sake. Amen.

GOOD NEWS OF GOD'S FORGIVING NATURE AND CLEANSING POWER

The saying is sure and worthy of full acceptance, that Christ Jesus came into the world to save sinners. By our own admission we are sinners. Through our confession, our desire for forgiveness and amendment come God's miracles of pardon and restoration. Praise God for his bountiful blessings!

GLORIA PATRI

CALL TO CONFESSION

Even our awareness of the calendar can become an avenue of sin into our lives. The twin goods of recollection and anticipation can hypnotize us, so that we do not see the crucial issues of today. From such sin, good Lord, deliver us.

CONFESSION

Silent, private.
In unison, aloud:

O God, our Father, you give us a sense of time, with memories of the past and promises for the future: Keep us ever mindful of the urgent importance of the present. We acknowledge that all too often we either treasure the past with nostalgia or impatiently await the future with longing. Forgive us such sinful ways. Focus afresh our energies on the present, the time for our full obedience to Jesus Christ, our Lord. Amen.

GOOD NEWS OF GOD'S FORGIVING NATURE AND CLEANSING POWER

God is tender and compassionate. As tenderly as a father treats his children, so God treats those who revere him. He takes our sins, confessed and repented of, farther away than the east is from the west. Praise God for mercifully pardoning us, for Jesus' sake!

GLORIA PATRI

CALL TO CONFESSION

We begin life as receivers and demanders. An infant can do little else. God's purpose for us is that we learn the joys of giving, giving until we can affirm the truth of Jesus' declaration: "It is more blessed to give than to receive." How often we revert to infantile behavior. From such recidivism, good Lord, deliver us.

CONFESSION

Silent, private.
In unison, aloud:

O God, our Father, you have freed us from the condition of always receiving, and you open to us the glories of giving—of our possessions and of ourselves: We acknowledge that all too often we relapse into the "gimme" syndrome. Forgive us such sinning. Enable us to be steady, cheerful, imaginative, resourceful givers, for the sake of Jesus, the greatest gift of all. Amen.

GOOD NEWS OF GOD'S FORGIVING NATURE AND CLEANSING POWER

God so loved the world that he gave his only begotten Son, that whosoever believes in him should not perish, but have everlasting life. Through the grace of our belief in Jesus we know the love of God and his will to forgive, his power to cleanse. Praise God for his continuing mercies to us!

GLORIA PATRI

CALL TO CONFESSION

"Cheap grace" is not part of the good news. A perfunctory "I'm sorry," with little intention of amending our ways, is presumptuous sin. If we desire pardon, we must expect cleansing; if we want forgiveness, we must be ready to take steady steps in the paths of righteousness. From flippant confession, good Lord, deliver us.

CONFESSION

Silent, private.
In unison, aloud:

O God, our Father, you give us the high privilege of confession of sin, and the marvelous promise of forgiveness, cleansing, and restoration in love: We acknowledge that all too often we neglect to recognize, and own, our rebellion against you, and our unconcern over our hurts of others. Forgive us our misuse of such treasure. Help us, more and more, to live wholesomely as responsive persons in our relationships with you, with others, and with ourselves, through Jesus Christ, our Lord. Amen.

GOOD NEWS OF GOD'S FORGIVING NATURE AND CLEANSING POWER

If we say we have no sin, we deceive ourselves and the truth is not in us. If we confess our sins, he is faithful and just to forgive our sins and to cleanse us from all unrighteousness. Thanks be to God, who merits our trust, accepts our confession, forgives us, and enables repentant sinners to grow in grace and in the knowledge of Christ Jesus, our Lord. Praise be to God!

GLORIA PATRI

CALLS TO CONFESSION, PRAYERS

CALL TO CONFESSION

How frequently we do what is right in our own eyes, forgetting we live in a universe that God designed and over which he is sovereign. How frequently we live as though physical death is final fact for us, when God has another word: resurrection. From such delusions, good Lord, deliver us.

CONFESSION

Silent, private.
In unison, aloud:

O God, our Father, you saw sin enter your creation when husband and wife disobeyed your command; you saw physical death enter when brother rose up and murdered brother: All too often we view sin as simple error and physical death as final fact. Forgive our rebellion; establish anew within us the assurance of your resurrecting power, through Jesus Christ, our Lord. Amen.

CALL TO CONFESSION

A motor firing on less than all cylinders is a cripple and a plague. When we fail to let the grace of our Lord Jesus Christ, the love of God, and the fellowship of the Holy Spirit steadily empower us, we live at a "poor, dying rate." From such malfunctioning, good Lord, deliver us.

CONFESSION

Silent, private.
In unison, aloud:

O God, our Father, you have put us in a grand and good universe of your creating, you have sent Jesus in your love to save us from the power of sin and dread of physical death, and you pour out the Holy Spirit upon your people to regenerate, enlighten, comfort, and empower them: We acknowledge that all too often we feel ourselves lost in an unfriendly environment and without power or direction. Forgive such gross sinning by us. Help us to rejoice in your love, to live gloriously by the Spirit, and to rest secure in grace, through Jesus Christ, our Savior. Amen.

CALL TO CONFESSION

A drowning person who does not grasp a life preserver thrown within reach and a trapped person who does not leap to the safety of a net are fools. If we do not receive God-given insight and wisdom through the Holy Spirit, we, likewise, are fools. From such stupidity, good Lord, deliver us.

CONFESSION

Silent, private.
In unison, aloud:

O God, our Father, you give us the marvelous gift of the enlightening Holy Spirit, for bringing truth and wisdom from the Holy Scripture, for granting revelations to guide us in solving problems, for seeing clearly the paths of righteousness: We acknowledge that all too often we neglect to appropriate such enlightenment, letting the Scripture lie silently before us, letting problems remain unsolved, letting the paths of righteousness be shrouded by rank overgrowth. Forgive our neglect of such treasure. Enable us, more and more, to open our minds to the Holy Spirit's witness, that we may live effectively as your useful people, through Jesus Christ, our Lord. Amen.

CALL TO CONFESSION

How often we know the daily Dow Jones averages, Heloise's latest hints, the current baseball batting averages, Ann Lander's recent advice, the disc jockeys' top forty tunes, soap opera plots up to the minute, and futures quoted on merchandise marts, but do not know God's plans and purposes, his promises and power as revealed in the Bible. From storage of such partial knowledge and neglect of such life-giving wisdom, good Lord, deliver us.

CONFESSION

Silent, private.
In unison, aloud:

O God, our Father, you give us minds to know you and to unlock your gifts within the universe for human good: We acknowledge that all too often we let our minds wander from such tasks; we fill them with trivia; we turn them to nefarious schemes. Forgive our misuse of such treasure. Help us apply our minds to understanding your Word and will, through Jesus Christ, our Lord. Amen.

CALL TO CONFESSION

How much we miss that is readily available to us, simply because we do not appropriate it: the beauties of sky and forest, meadows and window boxes; the joys of children's laughter, old people's reminiscences; the bountiful resources offered through the Holy Spirit. From such gross failure to enrich our lives, good Lord, deliver us.

CONFESSION

Silent, private.
In unison, aloud:

O God, our Father, you give us the marvelous gift of the empowering Holy Spirit, for the accomplishment of your purposes: We acknowledge that all too often we are fearful to open ourselves to this power. We limp along in life drawing upon poor substitutes for such power, or expect such power to be exercised by you through other persons. Forgive us our neglect of such treasure. Help us, more and more, to draw upon this marvelously energizing power, for the accomplishment of your glorious purposes, in and through us, for Jesus' sake. Amen.

CALL TO CONFESSION

Families are God's good plan for the begetting and nurturing of human beings. If we have been less than wholesome members of a family, we have sinned.

CONFESSION

Silent, private.
In unison, aloud:
O God, our Father, you give us the blessed gift of families, and also enfold us within the living body of Christ, the church: We acknowledge that all too often we are petulant, perfunctory, and perverse participants in our family life. Forgive us our misuse of such treasure. Help us to honor our parents, esteem our spouse, befriend our siblings, nurture our children, and to be useful members of this company of Jesus' disciples; by his mercy and for his sake. Amen.

CALL TO CONFESSION

Who among us is not an "outlaw"? How often we jaywalk, exceed speed limits, ooze through stop signs, fudge on traffic lights, cross a double stripe when passing. We also defy the laws of God. From such brazen arrogance, good Lord, deliver us.

CONFESSION

Silent, private.
In unison, aloud:

O God, our Father, you give us commandments, rules, admonitions by which to regulate our private lives, our interpersonal relationships, and our fellowship with you: We acknowledge that all too often we ignore them. We seek, rather, to make our own rules or to try to live just as we choose. Forgive our misuse of such treasure. Help us to follow with thanksgiving your laws which guide us in the paths of righteousness, for Jesus' sake. Amen.

CALL TO CONFESSION

When we acquire a new automobile, television set, microwave oven, sewing machine, boat and motor, we read with careful attention the accompanying manual so as to achieve maximum results. God gives us the priceless, irreplaceable gift of our bodies; yet, so often, we fail to consult his manual, the Bible, so as to achieve maximum results. From such mismanagement of valuable goods, good Lord, deliver us.

CONFESSION

Silent, private.
In unison, aloud:

O God, our Father, you give us bodies, intricately designed, delicately balanced, marvelously durable: We acknowledge that all too often we treat our bodies with disrespect. We fail to honor them as a temple of the Holy Spirit, and to use them as instruments to accomplish your will. Forgive our misuse of such treasure. Help us amend our negligent ways, through Jesus Christ, our Lord. Amen.

CALL TO CONFESSION

We are forgetful that we live daily among miracles and mysteries of God: saltwater from the seas dropped as fresh water over hill and dale, photosynthesis in plants harnessing the energy of the sun, new human lives of trust and hope for lives formerly consumed by sin and destined for destruction. From such insensitivity to infinite miracles and mysteries of divine providence, good Lord, deliver us.

CONFESSION

Silent, private.
In unison, aloud:
O God, our Father, you inspired Jesus to take ordinary bread and drink and give them a holy, sacramental significance: We confess that all too often we neither see nor feel such significance in what we eat. Forgive our frequent failure to give thanks to you for daily nourishment. Prepare us now to receive the Lord's Supper with hearts thankful for all your sustaining graces, through Jesus Christ, our Lord. Amen.

PRAYERS OF CONFESSION

O God, our Father, from you comes every good gift from the bounty of the land, from the resources of the sea, from the riches of the atmosphere, from the hearts and minds of neighbors and friends: We acknowledge that all too often we receive such blessings without returning thanks—to you or to others. Forgive us our sins of ingratitude. Aid us to receive with thanksgiving, and to give with glad hearts and generous hands, through Jesus Christ, our Lord. Amen.

• • •

O God, our Father, you hold us to account for our private actions; to you we confess and from you we receive gracious forgiveness: All too often we forget sins we commit together, as families, as citizens, as special groups, as a nation. Forgive each of us when we participate in such group sinning; and turn us, as groups, from our collective sinful ways, through Jesus Christ, our Lord. Amen.

• • •

O God, our Father, you surround us with your love, and with loving brothers and sisters in Christ; and you bind us supportively within the universal and eternal fellowship of the church: All too often we forget to reach out in enfolding love to the isolated, the refugee, the neglected, who do not know your saving love. Forgive our sin of failing to love other persons, even as we seek to love you, through Jesus Christ, our Lord. Amen.

• • •

O God, our Father, you give us joy to refresh us: We acknowledge that all too often we let joy curdle into jealousy, jealousy into envy, and envy leads us down and down until we feel neglected and despairing. Forgive our misuse of such treasure. Help us to receive joy, and enable us to help others to sing with us "Hallelujah!" through Jesus Christ, our Lord. Amen.

• • •

O God, our Father, you give us love to sweeten us: We acknowledge that all too often we let love sour into dislike, dislike into unconcern, unconcern into hate, and hate attacks us with physical distress and disease. Forgive our misuse of such treasure. Help us to receive your love for us, and let it keep us wholesomely loving, through Jesus Christ, our Lord. Amen.

• • •

O God, our Father, you give us peace to still our anxiety over sin and our dread of physical death: We acknowledge that all too often we let such personal peace be prostituted to unconcern over other evils pressing upon persons. Forgive our misuse of such treasure. Help us, in calm assurance of our salvation and eternal life, to fight with vigor and effectiveness battles against injustice, unkindness, and gross neglect, through Jesus Christ, our Lord. Amen.

• • •

O God, our Father, you give us mercy to make us tender toward others: We acknowledge that all too often we let mercy wither to justice, justice to vengeance, which makes us brittle and hard toward other persons. Forgive us our misuse of such treasure. Help us to receive mercy and to be more and more merciful to others, through Jesus Christ, our Lord. Amen.

• • •

O God, our Father, you give us hope to steady us in our earthly pilgrimage: We acknowledge that all too often we treasure hope and forget the pilgrimage, or we discard hope because of current darkness, or we shun hope and settle for present pleasures. Forgive our misuse of such treasure. Help us to fix our hearts anew on your exceeding great and precious promises on which hope rests, through Jesus Christ, our Lord. Amen.

• • •

O God, our Father, you give us faith to nourish our trust in you: We acknowledge that all too often we let our minds unsettle the faith our hearts know to be true, or we close our minds to doubt which can lead to strengthened faith, or we fix our faith on fallible substitutes. Forgive our misuse of such treasure. Enable us, using our hearts and minds, to make stronger and stronger the sinews of faith as we trust ourselves ever more completely to you alone, through Jesus Christ, our Lord. Amen.

• • •

O God, our Father, you give us feet to move about with purpose and direction upon the planet designed for our habitation: We acknowledge that all too often we prop up our feet in idleness or turn them from the paths of righteousness or stub them against the rocks of pride. Forgive us such misuse of treasure from you. Help us to walk uprightly in obedience and service, through Jesus Christ, our Lord. Amen.

• • •

O God, our Father, you give us ears to hear the sounds of splendor in your creation and the communications of our fellow human beings: We acknowledge that all too often we close our ears to the music of nature and to the pleas of our neighbor. Forgive us our misuse of such treasure. Help us to hear, above all the din about us, the cries of others to us, and also to hear your still, small voice of command, counsel, and comfort, through Jesus Christ, our Lord. Amen.

• • •

O God, our Father, you give us hands to serve you by serving one another: We acknowledge that all too often we ball our hands into fists for fighting, wring them together in perplexity or despair, or let them hang idly by our sides in apathy. Forgive our misuse of such treasure. Help us to stretch forth in usefulness our hands to family, friends, and neighbors, lifting burdens, healing hurts, producing good, through Jesus Christ, our Lord. Amen.

• • •

O God, our Father, you give us eyes to see beauty in your creation, to recognize family and friends, to read both your Word and the signs of the times: We acknowledge that all too often we let the myopia of selfishness or the astigmatism of limited interest blur our vision. Forgive our misuse of such treasure. Help us to see the world and the people in it with eyes wide open to evil and to good and to your plan of salvation, through Jesus Christ, our Lord. Amen.

• • •

O God, our Father, you give us mouths with which to taste and speak: We acknowledge that all too often we ingest that which is damaging to us and we speak forth that which is damaging to others. Forgive our misuse of such treasure. Grant that we may taste with new delight that which is good for our bodies and speak with graciousness all that will bless those near us, through Jesus Christ, our Lord. Amen.

• • •

O God, our Father, you give us noses with which to inhale life-giving oxygen and delight-giving aromas: We acknowledge that all too often we tilt our noses in hauteur, or stick them into others' business. Forgive our misuse of such treasure. Help us to seek out the delicate fragrances you have for us: lilac and lavender, honeysuckle and jasmine, new-mown hay and orange blossoms; to breathe in deeply, with thanksgiving, oxygen which sustains our bodily functions; and to be inspired, for our salvation, by the Holy Spirit; through Jesus Christ, our Lord. Amen.

• • •

O God, our Father, you have put us in a grand and good universe of your creating; in your love you have sent Jesus to save us from the power of sin and the dread of physical death; and you pour out the Holy Spirit upon your people to regenerate, enlighten, comfort, and empower: We acknowledge that all too often we feel ourselves lost in an unfriendly environment and without direction or power. Forgive such gross sinning by us. Help us to rejoice in your love, live gloriously by the Spirit, and rest secure in grace, through Jesus Christ, our Savior. Amen.

• • •

O God, our Father, you give Jesus as Lord, Sovereign over matter in its vastness, over human society in its diversity, over individuals in their incredible distinctiveness: We acknowledge that all too often we affirm his Lordship only within narrow aspects of our life—Sunday mornings, charitable acts, minor matters of private morality. Forgive us the sins of such limited allegiance. Help us, more and more, to be obedient to his Lordship in economic enterprise, political practice, educational endeavor, aesthetic experience, and uses of leisure, so that we can rightfully declare of him: "My Lord and my God!" Amen.

• • •

O God, our Father, you give and give and give, so that we can live: We acknowledge that all too often we receive and receive and receive only that we may have. Forgive our sins of selfishness. Help us—yes, by your gift of the Holy Spirit—to learn as your trusting children: to give and give and give, of ourselves and of things entrusted to us; to feed, clothe, and shelter the needy; to tell the good news to those who are lost; to heal those who are sick in body and spirit; to liberate the oppressed, that we may be agents of your blessings to them; through Jesus Christ, our Lord. Amen.

• • •

O God, our Father, you give us the marvelous gift of parents, to nurture us, to shepherd us, and to prepare us for self-directed lives beyond the home: We acknowledge that all too often we fail to return their love, to honor their trust, to gladden them with even minor expressions of appreciation. Forgive us such sinning. Help us not only to honor them but also warmly to love those through whom you have given us the gift of life, through Jesus Christ, our Lord. Amen.

• • •

O God, our Father, you have given us brothers and sisters in our biological families, and also in the household of faith, even within this congregation: We acknowledge that all too often we feel toward them hostility, not love; animosity, not mercy; superiority, not equality; annoyance, not acceptance. Forgive our sin. Help us fully and faithfully to learn to love these, our nearest neighbors, as ourselves, through Jesus Christ, our Lord. Amen.

• • •

O God, our Father, you give us neighbors in various sizes and shapes, needs and expectations, and you require that we reach out to them in self-giving love: We acknowledge that, at their approach, we all too often turn our backs, divert our eyes, fold our hands, and hobble our feet. Forgive us such sinning. Help us, more and more, to reach out to our neighbors with our hearts in our hands and with the good news on our lips, through Jesus Christ, our Lord. Amen.

• • •

O God, our Father, you surround us with wholesome, helpful teachers in homes and schools, in colleges and various continuing education opportunities; and you have given us minds with which to learn truth, to appreciate beauty, and to advance the good: We acknowledge that all too often we scorn faithful teachers by inattention and unpreparedness. Forgive us such sin. Help us in public school, in Sunday school, in all constructive classes, to use our minds well and to equip ourselves better to be useful in your kingdom's work, through Jesus Christ, our Lord. Amen.

• • •

O God, our Father, you send Jesus to call us, one by one, into exciting, challenging, useful discipleship: We acknowledge that all too often we duck his summons, or say "Yes" and mean "Maybe," or enlist and then seek to give orders rather than to obey his commands. Forgive our failures to be trustworthy disciples. Help us, here and now, to respond in earnest and expectant commitment, through Jesus Christ, our Lord. Amen.

• • •

O God, our Father, you beam upon us the life-giving, life-sustaining light through Jesus: We acknowledge that all too often we hunt for the shadows, and choose to walk in darkness. Forgive our failures to claim and to enjoy blessings you provide for our guidance. Help us, more and more, to follow the Light, and to reflect that Light, so that others, too, may walk in joy, security, and usefulness, through Jesus Christ, our Lord. Amen.

• • •

O God, our Father, you give us both barriers to overcome and openings to high adventure: We acknowledge that all too often we cringe before the barriers and shun the opportunities. Forgive our cowardly sin. Help us to draw boldly on resources you make available for surmounting barriers and for moving along high roads to great achievement, through Jesus Christ, our Lord. Amen.

• • •

O God, our Father, you surround us with an abundance of things—some life-sustaining or life-enriching, some life-encumbering; and you also enable us to find life abundant through blessings of your love, your grace, your reconciling forgiveness: We acknowledge that all too often we frantically seek things in abundance and faint for lack of receiving these other mercies from you. Forgive our debilitating sinning. Help us to receive proper things with gratitude, and to share them; but evermore help us to accept your other gifts and everlasting life they make possible; through Jesus Christ, our Lord. Amen.

• • •

O God, our Father, you give us the treasure of uniqueness in our own individual selves: We acknowledge that all too often we value our selves too little, we apologize for our selves too frequently, we conform our selves too easily to others. Forgive us such sin. Help us to affirm our selves as your special creations, and to seek to be and to do all you have designed for us, through Jesus Christ, our Lord. Amen.

• • •

O God, our Father, you give us the assurance of your power and love through the resurrection of Jesus from the tomb, and you free us in this life from the deadly grip of sin's awesome power: We acknowledge that all too often we still face our impending physical death with dread. Forgive us such sin. Help us to live our present life with rejoicing and usefulness, and to contemplate the future with calm assurance, confident that you will bring us to eternal fellowship and joy, through Jesus Christ, our Lord. Amen.

• • •

A GUIDE TO THE CONTENTS
KEY PHRASES

CALLS TO WORSHIP

PRAYERS FOR SPECIAL DAYS AND OCCASIONS

CONFESSION

CALLS TO CONFESSION, PRAYERS OF CONFESSION, GOOD NEWS

CALLS TO CONFESSION AND PRAYERS OF CONFESSION

PRAYERS OF CONFESSION